Veronica's Veil

Poems, Prayers, and Promises

of the

Holy Face Devotion

by

Donna Sue Berry

Edited by
Eugenia Zanone

Illustrations by
Jane Frances Privett

Berry Books Publishing

D0839016

Berry Books Publishing
PO Box 30661
Edmond, Oklahoma
73003

ISBN 978-0-692-07889-1

THIS LITTLE DEVOTIONAL BOOK IS
COMPILED AND BASED ON PAPAL BRIEFS
BOOKS ABOUT THE
HOLY FACE DEVOTION
THE AUTOBIOGRAPHIES
OF
SISTER MARIE DE ST. PIERRE
AND VENERABLE LEO DUPONT
WITH IMPRIMATUR
AND
HISTORICAL RECORDS

DECLARATION

We hereby declare, that we absolutely and entirely conform to the decree of Urban VIII, with respect to the terms of eulogy or veneration applied to the servant of God, Sister Marie de St. Pierre, and other pious persons, as well as to the divine revelations mentioned in the present book; and moreover, that we by no means anticipate the decisions of the Holy See.

Acknowledgement

To Everyone
who has ever shared the

Most Beautiful Work Under Heaven

The Work of Reparation
Through
Devotion to the Holy Face

VERA EFFIGIES SACRI VULTUS DOMINI NOSTRI JESU CHRISTI

Dedicated
to the
Eternal Father
in
Reparation

for

Sins of Blasphemy
Crimes of Communists
Profanation of Sundays
and
Holy Days of Obligation

Promises
of
Our Lord Jesus Christ
in favor of all who honor
His Holy Face

1. 'They shall receive in themselves, by the impression of My Humanity, a bright irradiation from My Divinity, and shall be so illuminated by it in their inmost souls that by their likeness to My Face they shall shine with a brightness surpassing that of many others in eternal life.' (St. Gertrude, book iv. Ch. vii.)

2. St. Mechtilde having asked our Lord that those who celebrate the memory of His sweet Face should ever be deprived of His amiable company, He replied: '**Not one of them shall be separated from me.**' (St. Mechtilde, De la Grace Spirituelle, book i. ch. xiii.)

3. *'Our Lord'*, said Sister Marie de St. Pierre, *'has promised me that He will imprint His Divine likeness on the souls of those who honor His Most Holy Countenance.'* (**January 21st, 1847.**)

4. *'This Adorable Face is, as it were, the seal of the Divinity, which has the virtue of reproducing the likeness of God in the souls that are applied to it.'* Sister Saint Marie de St. Pierre (**November 6, 1845.**)

5. 'By My Holy Face you shall work miracles.' (October 27th, 1845.)

6. 'By My Holy Face you will obtain the conversion of many sinners. Nothing that you ask in making this offering will be refused to you. No one can know how pleasing the sight of My Face is to My Father!' (November 22nd, 1846.)

7. 'As in a kingdom you can procure all you wish for with a coin marked with the prince's effigy, so in the kingdom of Heaven you will obtain all you desire with the precious coin of my Holy Humanity, which is My Adorable Countenance.' (October 29th, 1845.)

8. 'All those who honor My Holy Face in a spirit of Reparation will, by so doing, perform the office of the pious Veronica.' (October 27th, 1845.)

9. 'According to the care you take in making Reparation to My Face, disfigured by blasphemies, so will I take care of your soul which has been disfigured by sin. I will reprint My image and render it as beautiful as it was on leaving the baptismal font.' (November 3, 1845.)

10. *'Our Lord has promised me for all those who defend His cause in this Work of Reparation, by words, by prayers, or in writing, that He will defend them before His Father; at their death He will purify their souls by effacing all the blots of sin and will restore to them their primitive beauty.'* Sister Marie de St. Pierre (March 12th, 1846.)

Vera Effigies Sacri Vultus Domini Nostri Jesu Christi
quæ Romæ in Sacrosancta Basilica S. Petri in Vaticano religiosissime observatur et colitur

Let God arise, and let His enemies be scattered,
and let them that hate Him flee from before His face.

PS.67.3.

Table of Contents

Veronica, O Veronica,
such a pious deed you've done,
upon the road to Calvary,
a crown you've surely won!

dsb

That Day in Jerusalem AD 33 . . .

The crowd in the city was immense and growing angrier and more uncontrollable as their blood thirstiness increased for the man carrying his cross. Their screams for his crucifixion, curses, and hatred resonated throughout the streets of Jerusalem, and few, it seemed, could be found wanting him to live.

Standing on a corner, just off the main street, she maintained a safe distance while watching the mob build. She was so scared and afraid that they would want to harm her and his other followers who were watching, that she couldn't keep from shaking. Just up the street, she saw the crowd parting and the first of the Roman soldiers as they led their prisoner to his death.

She had to see him. She had to get closer to him. Her life had changed because of the teacher from Nazareth. So, she pushed through the crowd to be nearer to him and darted around some men who had paused to throw rocks at the prisoner. Quickly, she brushed past some women slinging filthy insults towards him, and she pulled her veil further down on her forehead to partially cover her face so as not to be recognized. Then stepping through an opening in the throng, she found herself at the edge of the street and right behind a soldier holding back the crowd.

Looking to her left, she saw Jesus. He was only a few feet away now, and he would soon pass right in front of her. Her heart almost stopped as she saw him. This was no man trudging slowly up the hill to Calvary; this was a massive open wound! From head to toe his flesh was torn. His blood, both dried and flowing, covered his clothing. A crown of thorns adorned his head. It had been put there by one of his evil torturers to mock him and to make sure he felt as much pain as possible.

Suddenly, she jumped as the man next to her shouted obscenities and threw a large rock at Jesus. As it struck him, he stumbled and collapsed to the ground under the heavy cross; man and wood crashing down against the cobbled stones.

This was her chance! She lurched forward past the guard and onto the ground in front of Jesus, sliding her veil from her head as she did. Looking up into his face, she saw her 'Redemption'! His eyes penetrated hers with such compassion and tenderness that the scene around her simply disappeared, and the only sound she heard was his breathing. She raised her veil towards him, and he achingly, painfully wiped his face covered with blood, sweat, dust, and spittle.

Instantly she was wrenched away from him by a soldier and flung back into the raging sea of people clamoring for his death. They pulled her hair and hit at her as she pushed and shoved her way through them, fighting to get away. Clutching the veil close to her chest, she didn't stop until the din was far behind her, and she had found a darkened doorway in which to rest. Finally, alone, she sank to the ground, legs trembling, not only from the danger she had felt, but from the impact of what she had done. AND - his eyes. Those eyes. She had seen love and salvation in those eyes! She had felt his intense love!

Aware of her clenched fists still holding the veil tightly, she loosened her grip and gasped at what she saw. Upon the cloth, miraculously, was the image of his face. Tears sprang from her eyes as she beheld his blood drawn features looking back at her, knowing that his image would be imprinted on her soul forever.

Emotional and overwhelmed by what she saw, she slowly, ever so slowly, bent her head toward the blood-stained veil to kiss her Savior's cheek …

"I seek Veronicas!"

Jesus to Sr. Marie de St. Pierre

Santa Veronica con il velo
Mattia Preti (1613-1699)

Veronica's Veil

Veronica could not compete
With the roaring, raucous mob,
Though no one heard her plea to move,
She pushed with one last sob.

Compassion and persistence,
Had begged her try again,
And just that quick she found herself
Before the man condemned.

It's then He fell beneath the cross,
that forced Him to the ground,
Which ripped His skin and tore His face,
Head pierced by thorny crown.

Blood mixing with the dirt and stones,
They spat upon Him too,
This cursed man whom they reviled,
As winds of hatred blew.

But quickly moving to His side,
She felt a sudden chill,
The world around her disappeared,
And time itself stood still.

She slid her veil from off her head,
And with it cupped His face,
A touching act of mercy in
Response to heaven's grace.

Then as she pulled the veil away,
A tear ran down her cheek,
His look of love made her cry out,
And made her knees grow weak.

His sacred eyes, His holy face,
His body racked with pain,
A memory she'd not forget,
Long after He was slain.

But soldiers then wrenched her away,
Into the screaming crowd.
She clawed and shoved her way through them,
Heart pounding with head bowed.

At last she found a quiet street,
And knelt in sheer relief.
The bloody veil clutched to her chest,
She cried from fear and grief.

Then as she held the veil she saw
The imprint of His face,
Majestic in Its blood and wounds,
The source of every grace.

The image burned upon her soul,
She found she could not speak,
But bowed in adoration as
She kissed her Savior's cheek.

Who is Saint Veronica

She is called Veronica, the compassionate woman who took pity on Christ when she saw Him fall beneath the weight of the wooden cross, and who watched His bloody body racked from torture; His face covered with blood, sweat, and spittle as He carried His cross up the hill to Calvary to die. Courageously, using her veil to wipe away the blood and muck, she was rewarded by the image of His face impressed upon the cloth; a sign of Jesus' gratitude for her mercy. *But who was she*, and where did she come from? The Catholic Church says she is a saint whose Feast Day is celebrated February 4th on the old Church calendar and July 12th on the current one, and she is recognized as the woman in the sixth Station of the Cross.

There is no mention of her or this story in the Gospels. It is only through Catholic tradition, early Church history, the apocryphal *Acts of Pilate*, and private revelations, that the story of this pious woman, her act of compassion, and the miraculous image of Christ's face upon her veil became known. It is written that she was a woman of position and the wife of Sirach, one of the counselors belonging to the temple, and that she was approximately 50 years of age at the time that Christ was crucified.

Private revelations posit that her given Jewish name may have been Seraphia. Whether that is her given name or not, the Church, as well as Our Lord in revelations to Sr. Marie de St. Pierre, a Carmelite nun of Tours, France in 1843, have named her by the title of "her office." Our Lord's words to Sr. Marie de St. Pierre, when he spoke of Veronica, *per se* what she did for him in that reparatory act, and then in the promise that he gave, refer to what she did "*as an office.*"

> All those who honor My Face in a spirit of
> reparation will, by doing so, perform *the office*
> of the pious Veronica.

Additionally, in the Eastern Church, the name Veronica, which means 'true-image', also translates as Bernice. The name 'Veronica' itself is a Latinisation of Berenice (Greek: Βερενίκη, *Berenikē,* with a secondary form *Beronike*), a Macedonian name, meaning **'bearer of Victory'**. The woman who offered her veil to Jesus was known by this name in the Byzantine East, but in the Latin West the name took a life of its own. The possibility of her given Jewish name being *Seraphia* or *Berenice*, either of these names reflect **the high office** to which Veronica was called.

It is the Seraphic rank of angels, the Seraphim angels being the highest order, who eternally and constantly praise God to His Face. The name Berenice – bearer of victory – signifies that the veil she carried is the sign of victory – the suffering Face of Christ and then the glorified Face which we will see at His Coming.

In 1885, the *Dublin Review* wrote:
> [...] The legends of St. Veronica tell us that she was a
> noble Jewess, Seraphia by name, of sacerdotal race, daughter
> of a brother of Zachary of Hebron; consequently, cousin
> to St. John the Baptist. She was five years older than the
> Blessed Virgin, with whom she had been raised among
> the Maidens of the Temple, and formed with her a close
> friendship, and was present at her espousal with St. Joseph.
> She was also related to the aged Simeon, and had shared
> his eager longings for the advent of the Messiah. When

Jesus, at twelve years of age, remained behind in the
Temple amid the doctors, Seraphia gave Him hospitality
and nourishment in a house situated near the Bethlehem
gate, a quarter of a league from Jerusalem, where He remained
when not within the Temple limits, [...]

In the apocryphal *Acts of Pilate*, Pilate associates this woman as being
the same woman mentioned in the New Testament with the flow of
blood who was cured by touching the hem of Jesus' cloak.

The veil, mentioned in medieval texts by Father John van Bolland
(1596-1665), whose name was adopted by the Bollandists, the Jesuit
editor of the Acta Sanctorum, writes that, "It is the unanimous
opinion of all sacred historians and the firm belief of all true
Christians that the veil is the identical and veritable cloth offered to
the Redeemer on his way to Calvary." The Bollandists, in an old
church missal, have a Mass, "DE S. Veronica seu Vultus Domini".

Matthew of Westminster speaks of the imprint of the image of the
Savior, which is called Veronica, in *Effigies Domenici vultus quae Veronica
nuncupatur*. The veil is even mentioned in Dante's, *The Divine Comedy*,
Paradise, XXXI, 104, and in the *Vita Nuova*, 40, 1 (Catholic
Encyclopedia).

In the 1870 book, *Historical Notice of the Veronica, or The Holy Face of Our
Lord Jesus Christ*, it is written that:

From a constant tradition, which is founded in the most
authentic documents, we are informed, that whilst Our
Saviour was on the painful journey to Calvary, loaded
with the heavy wood of the cross, the altar on which He
was to sacrifice His life for the redemption of mankind,
a holy woman, moved by compassion, presented Him
a handkerchief, or towel, to wipe His face, all covered with
sweat, spittle, dust, and blood; and that Jesus, having used it,
gave it back to her having impressed on it His majestic
and venerable image, so full of the deep sorrow into which

He was then plunged by the weight of the sins of the world.
It is for this reason, that this holy woman is usually represented near Our Saviour, holding in her hands her veil with the Holy Face, as may be seen in the sixth station of the Station of the Cross.

An ailing Tiberius Caesar, according to tradition, having learned about the cloth with Jesus' face upon it, sent out messengers to collect everything they could about the life, death, resurrection, and ascension of Jesus, and had invited Veronica to come to Rome. When Veronica showed the emperor the veil, he was immediately cured of his malady. She remained in Rome, living there during the same time as Saints Peter and Paul.

The learned Piazza, in his work entitled, *Emerologio di Roma*, which was published in 1713, relates this pious story on the feast of St. Veronica, celebrated then on the 4th of February (Now on July 12th).

> St. Veronica, a noble lady of Jerusalem, lived about the year 38, of the Christian era, during the reign of the Emperor Tiberius. It is believed that she is the woman that was cured of the bloody flux by our Lord, and whom Baronius calls Berenicia, being called Veronica, from the circumstance of her having possessed the blessed relic of the Holy Face.

> After Jesus had left the house of Pilate, and was on His way to Calvary to be put to death, being all covered with blood from the scourges which He had received, and the wounds of His blessed temples, which were caused by the crown of sharp thorns; after having gone 450 steps, He came near to a house which formed an angle, where, Veronica seeing Him approach in the distance, through compassion, went to meet Him, and taking the veil from off her head, presented it to Him to wipe His face, all covered with sweat and blood. Our Lord benignly received it from her hands, having wiped His face with it, returned it to her with the impress of His Holy Face printed on it.

Veronica is said to have eventually bequeathed the veil to St. Clement I, St. Peter's third successor as Pope, and it was kept hidden in the depths of the catacombs during the three centuries of Christian persecution. Later it was placed in the church built over St. Peter's tomb (which was transformed into St. Peter's Basilica).

In 1208, Pope Innocent III instituted a procession which took place the first Sunday after the octave of Epiphany in which the Holy Face was carried solemnly from the basilica to the church at the hospital of the Holy Spirit, followed by cardinals and the Pope. Pope Innocent III gave a sermon to those present and three 'deniers' to each of a thousand poor foreigners, and three hundred to the hospital.

For this epic occasion, medals were struck bearing the representation of the Holy Face and the keys of St. Peter. The medals were called Veronicas, and pilgrims who visited the tombs of the holy Apostles wore them with great devotion. Even the pontifical money was impressed with the effigy of the Holy Face. Pope Innocent had prayers composed to the Holy Face and ordered them to be recited before the veil of St. Veronica, attaching to them certain indulgences.

Years later, the Holy Face was translated to the new St. Peter's Basilica on December 23rd, 1625, under the pontificate of Urban VIII, where the veil is preserved and protected by a crystal and gilt framed reliquary within a small chapel constructed in one of the four pillars that support the cupola of St. Peter's. Carefully guarded against deterioration or vandalism, it is displayed on 'Veronica's Pier,' or the balcony above her statue, which happens the four days of Holy week and Easter Sunday through the Monday of Pentecost. The huge statue of St. Veronica, created by Francesco Mochi (1629-1640), is situated in the niche of one of the piers supporting the main dome of the basilica and stands 16 feet tall. The artist captured Veronica's movement in stone as her extended arms sweep upwards holding the veil as if in her excitement to show off the cloth with Christ's face upon it.

At the base of the statue is a door which leads to two corridors, one leading down into the Vatican grottoes where the relics of St. Peter repose, and the other leads up through the interior of the niche where the Holy Veil resides. The Canons of St. Peter (entrusted with the guardianship and care of the Icon) have affixed three locks to the vault with three separate keys to protect the holy treasure.

From princes to powerful kings, many have often made their way in pilgrimage to Rome to venerate the Holy Face imprinted upon the veil of St. Veronica. They have been seen to lay down their scepter and crown, and to put on the surplice and rochet of the Canons of Saint Peter and to venerate on their knees the most holy relic covered in the sweat and the blood of the Savior.

Along the Via Dolorosa in Jerusalem the spot, where Veronica wiped Christ's Face, is still held in great veneration and represents the sixth Station of the Cross:

> Veronica's house stands on a street corner, and from the spot
> where she met Jesus to the Judiciary Gate, where he fell
> for the second time beneath His Cross, Christ proceeded
> three hundred and thirty-six paces and eleven feet. Henry
> Maundrell, writing in 1697, enumerates, amid the places
> pointed out to him along 'the Dolorous Way,' 'fourthly,

the spot where St. Veronica presented to Christ the handkerchief to wipe His bleeding brows.' Whilst a more recent traveler, the late Protestant Episcopal Bishop of New York, Dr. Wainwright, visiting the Holy Land in 1849, speaks of this house of Veronica, or, more correctly, the spot on which stood that house, the very ruins whereof have disappeared, and whereon is now seen the dwelling of a Greek family. You are shown the place where the heroic woman, forcing her way through the soldiers and the crowd which surrounded Jesus and casting herself at His feet, wiped his distorted features, the impression whereof was left upon the cloth which had touched the august Face of the Saviour of the world. This house of Veronica is about one hundred paces from the Judgment Gate, through which malefactors passed to be executed on Calvary. Behind the gate is the upright stone pillar whereon was posted the sentence of Pilate.

House of St. Veronica in Jerusalem 1900-1920

But a seal of authority, far more venerable, lies in the fact that the house of Veronica is numbered by the Church amongst the "Holy Places." A Bull of Pius IV, dated July 14th, 1561, "confirms and ratifies the Indulgences set forth on a handsome tablet, preserved near the most holy Sepulchre of the Lord Jesus Christ," which Sixtus V, Benedict XIII,

and Gregory XVI, successively recognized and published.
In the nomenclature of the Holy Places, to which the indulgences
are attached, as appearing on this tablet, reproduced in
the Bullarium of the Holy Land, we read:

**At the house of St. Veronica,
an indulgence of seven
years and seven quarantines.**

This Station is preserved in the pious exercise known as the
'Way of the Cross'.

The Veil

For just a moment she'd been there, directly in His gaze,
And handing Him her linen scarf, He'd wiped His bloody face.
Though her veil was meant to help Him, it caused more pain instead,
By catching on the thorny crown, encircling His head.

In pain He'd handed back her veil, hands shaking as He did,
His eyes expressing tender love through bruised and swollen lids.
So captivated by His look, she couldn't hear the sound
Of the chaos all around her as she knelt upon the ground.

Motionless on the rocky road, her heartbeat nearly stilled,
Recognizing God before her, this man who'd soon be killed.
Suddenly, hard and calloused hands had gripped her upper arms,
Which tore her gaze from off His face, and from that crown
of thorns.

Then flinging her into the crowd, a soldier jeered with glee,
With hatred on his evil face, all she could do was flee.
Once past the cruel and angry mob, she'd still no time to rest,
But had to hide outside the horde, fear building in her chest.

She stumbled to a doorway just as darkness filled the sky,
And crouched beside a wooden door where mournfully she cried.
Emotion overtaking her, she soon began to shake
While trembling fingers held the cloth that wiped her Savior's face.

"O Jesus," was her silent cry, "now what are we to do?
How will we live in dreadful fear or survive without You?"
Collapsing on the stone-cold ground, she shuddered from the chill,
Remembering just how He looked, she tightly hugged her veil.

And staring at the bloody cloth, she ceased to make a sound,
For what she saw upon her scarf made her heart start to pound!
It was her Savior and her Lord; she saw His Holy Face,
Imprinted there upon the veil, a miracle of grace.

The weight of His expression and His agonizing pain,
She knew that she would not forget nor ever see again.
So, she knelt before the image, the icon of her Lord,
She cupped the veil, inclined her head, and bent down to adore.

©2018 Donna Sue Berry

Devotees of the Holy Face

Since the moment of His birth, people have adored and loved the face of Christ. From the very first time that His Mother, the Blessed Virgin Mary, kissed His tiny newborn face, to that moment just before He disappeared into the clouds at His Ascension, multitudes on earth adored the beauty of His earthly countenance. Once He was hidden from their eyes, they carried the image of Christ in their hearts, imprinted upon their souls.

Just as then, His earthly body hidden from view, certain faithful throughout the centuries have had special devotion to the Holy Face of Jesus. Whether their meditation was on the face of the resurrected Christ, brilliant as the sun and radiant with glory, or in deep contemplation of His face, battered and bruised during His passion and death, devotees of the Holy Face imitate the Mother of God in venerating her Son.

Saint Bernard of Clairvaux, (d. 1153), in words attributed to him in the hymn, *O Sacred Head,* composed a remembrance of the Holy Passion of Christ beginning with those wounds located on the face and head of Christ.

O Sacred Head surrounded
By crown of piercing thorn!
O bleeding Head so wounded,
Reviled and put to scorn.

Death's pallid hue comes o'er Thee,
The glow of life decays,
Yet angel-hosts adore Thee,
And tremble as they gaze.

St. Mechtilde (1241-1298) had a great love for the Holy Face and the Most Holy Wounds of Christ. Conversing with her sisters she once told them, 'Let us all, full of holy desire, hasten to venerate the sweetest Countenance of Our Lord, which will in Heaven be our all, all that a glorified soul can desire...' And asking Christ to grant that those who contemplate His Holy Face would never be deprived of His amiable company, the Lord replied:

Not one of them shall be separated from Me. The
Splendor of My Countenance will be their eternal
rejoicing. Let men meditate with profound gratitude,
and keep always in their memory the acts of virtue I
practiced while on earth, all the sufferings and injuries
I bore during thirty-three years, the destitution in which
I received the affronts I had to bear from My own

creatures, and at last My death on the Cross, that most bitter death, born for love of man. By it, I bought his soul with My Precious Blood to make it My spouse. Let each one have as much love and gratitude for all these benefits as if I had suffered them for his salvation alone.

St. Gertrude the Great (1256-1302) often meditated upon the sufferings of Christ during His Passion and particularly, His Holy Face, wounded and disfigured by the torture which He endured. Once while contemplating His Adorable Face, covered with blood and spittle, she asked Him for a special grace for those who would practice this devotion. She heard Him say:

> All those who meditate frequently on the vision
> of My Divine Face, attracted by the desires of love,
> shall receive within them, through My Humanity, a
> bright ray of My Divinity, which shall enlighten their
> inmost souls so that they shall reflect the light of
> My Countenance in a special manner throughout
> all Eternity.

Blessed Columba Marmion, O.S.B. (1858-1923) wrote that: '... it is sometimes good to stretch one's hands out to the Lord and to look at Him with faith. This is a way of showing Him the depths of the soul that His eyes may penetrate the abysses into the hidden recesses of the heart. This kind of prayer is pure and very powerful, as that of a child that gazes into the father's face seeking his good pleasure: Seek ye the Lord, seek His Face EVERMORE!'

O Lord,
I seek Thy Holy Face!

St. Therese of the Child Jesus and the Holy Face (1873-1897), along with her entire family, became members of the Archconfraternity of Reparation to the Holy Face at Tours, France. She had a deep devotion to the Holy Face and a deep love for Sr. Marie de St. Pierre, a Carmelite nun from Tours, to whom our Lord gave the mission of promoting the Work of Reparation to His Holy Face. St. Therese wore a relic of Sr. Marie's hair, and kept a picture of the nun in her New Testament which she kept close to her heart. St. Therese of the Child Jesus was so devoted to the Holy Face that she was given permission to add this title to her name in Religious life. She even composed a prayer to the Holy Face:

O Jesus, who in Thy Bitter Passion didst become 'the most abject of men, and a man of sorrow', I venerate Thy Sacred Face whereon there once did shine the beauty and sweetness of the God head; but now it has become for me, as if it were, the face of a leper! Nevertheless, under those disfigured features, I recognize Thy Infinite Love, and I am consumed with the desire to love Thee and make Thee loved by all men. The tears that Thou hast shed so abundantly appear to me as so many precious pearls that I love to gather up, in order to purchase the souls of poor sinners by means of their infinite value. O Jesus, whose Adorable Face ravishes my heart, I implore Thee to fix deep within me Thy Divine Image, to set me on fire with Thy Love, and to make me worthy to contemplate in Heaven Thy Glorious Face. Amen.

Eternal Father,
I offer Thee the most
Holy Face of Thy Divine Son
to appease Thy wrath!

Sr. Marie de St. Pierre, O.C.D., a Carmelite nun in Tours, France from November 12th, 1839 – July 8th, 1848, was the recipient of a series of revelations from Christ who made known to her His desire for a particular and powerful devotion which he wished to be established throughout the world concerning reparation to His Holy Face. He asked that reparation be made for the numerous sins of blasphemies and profanities that take place constantly in the world, and He told her that this devotion would appease the anger of His Father. By means of this devotion, the faithful would be able to appeal to God for anything that they wished. Primarily the Devotion to the Holy Face consists of prayers given to Sr. Marie de St. Pierre by our Lord.

My Name is everywhere blasphemed, even
children blaspheme It! This frightful sin, more than
all others, grievously wounds My Divine Heart;
through blasphemy the sinner curses Me to My Face,
attacks Me openly, annihilates My redemption, and
himself pronounces his own condemnation and
his judgement. Blasphemy is a *poisoned arrow*
which continually wounds My Heart. I will give you a
golden arrow wherewith to wound It delightfully and
to heal the wounds inflicted on It by the malice of sinners.

He dictated to her the formula for act of praise and reparation:

The Golden Arrow Prayer

May the most holy, most sacred,
most adorable, most incomprehensible
and unutterable Name of God
be always praised, blessed, loved,
adored, and glorified in Heaven,
on earth, and under the earth,
by all the creatures of God,
and by the Sacred Heart of Our Lord,
Jesus Christ, in the most
Holy Sacrament of the Altar.
Amen.

Jesus, Himself, assured her that each time she repeated this act of praise, the Golden Arrow, that she would be wounding His Heart with a wound of love. Over the course of five years, Jesus gave many revelations and prayers to the nun who shared them in obedience with her Superiors, and shortly before she died, she relayed them to the local bishop in Tours. She was also able to share the revelations and information with a good friend of the Carmelites, Monsieur Leo Dupont (now Venerable).

Venerable Leo Dupont, (1797-1876) known as the Holy Man of Tours, was a very devout Catholic man, widower and father. He had practiced as an attorney and was a legal advisor and friend of the Carmelite Monastery in Tours and a devotee of the Holy Face. It was in his home, after receiving a copy of the Face of Christ on the Veil of Veronica from the Carmelites, that he hung it in his parlor with an oil lamp burning before it. He created a small domestic oratory with the image of Christ's Face as the center of his devotion. It is through Venerable Dupont's unwavering sacrifice and work of propagating the Holy Face Devotion, that it was established first in Tours, France and then worldwide, as authorized by Pope Leo XIII in 1885.

Aspirations

O Jesus, Son of Mary,
Who hast been crowned with cruel thorns,
grant that we may arrive at union with Thee.
Jesus, Son of Mary,
Who hast three times
inclined Thy Divine Face to the earth
in the Garden of Olives,
deign to incline towards the earth of my heart,
and water it with Thy tears, Thy Sweat,
and Thy Most Precious Blood!
Spirit of Love, Tongue of fire,
impress upon my heart the thrice
Holy Name of God!

Sister Marie de St. Pierre
October 4th, 1816 – July 8th, 1848

"According to the care you will take to make reparation to My Face, disfigured by blasphemy, will I take care of your soul disfigured by sin. I will reimprint My likeness upon it and make it as beautiful as when it came forth from the baptismal font...I alone Am the 'healer of souls,' I alone can renew in them the image of God, effaced by sin."
Jesus

Most Admirable is the Name
Of God

Who is Sr. Marie de St. Pierre

Little Francoise Perrine Eluére was born on October 4th, 1816 in Rennes, France to very devout Catholic parents whose love and instruction in the Catholic Faith caused her to fall in love with Jesus and to desire to become a Bride of Christ. Her mother cultivated in her small child a great love for the Blessed Mother, and her father taught her the Catholic Faith and the practice of making the Stations of the Cross.

Perrine was a sickly child, and because of her parent's indulgently pampering their daughter, she became very precocious. But through their discipline and prayer, and her own devotion to the Virgin Mary, she overcame her temper and moodiness, and learned how to make sacrifices to change her impatience, often turning her thoughts to God, saying: 'My God, I offer Thee this in reparation for my sins.'

Her prayer life grew, and soon mental prayer was where she spent a lot of her time, meditating upon God and on the suffering and passion of Jesus. She came to realize how much her own sins had hurt the heart of her Savior, and doubt and scruples began to plague her. But after hearing a sermon on mental prayer, she received the grace to grow in love and confidence in her prayer life, and soon she was skillfully adept in the way of the saints.

Perrine's beloved mother died when she was twelve years old, just as St. Teresa of Avila's had. And just like St. Teresa, she threw herself at the feet of the Blessed Mother begging the Virgin to take her as her own daughter and to become her mother. Our Lady did, in fact, and kept Perrine close to her Immaculate Heart the rest of her life.

As she grew up, Perrine's aunts took care of her, teaching her not only by their pious examples of Catholicity, but teaching her the fine art of dressmaking in their shop. Perrine did exquisite work even though she maintained a constant interior conversation with the Lord, frequently made Spiritual Communions which transported her so strongly during her work that she found it difficult not to show her emotions and excitement. Her aunts set aside a corner of the shop for her to do her work in; a quiet place that would help in not disturbing the other employees and kept them from seeing the workings of grace in her soul.

One of her aunts was a superior of the Congregation of the Most Blessed Virgin, a congregation established for working girls where no vows were taken, but which gave them rules to follow that were intended to help preserve piety in the hearts of the young women who were members. Perrine was accepted into the congregation after completing a time of probation, and on the day of her admittance she was dressed all in white and carried a large, lighted candle while she made her Act of Consecration.

It was shortly after she was admitted into the congregation that her period of spiritual consolations and joy seemed to dry up. In her own words she wrote:

Our Lord, having nourished me now for quite a long
time with the milk of consolations, wished to give me
a more solid nourishment in order to strengthen my soul.
He made me pass from Thabor to Calvary. The Divine Savior
withdrawing His consolations now abandoned me to
spiritual dryness and interior aridity. This state seemed
very strange to me. Alas, not to feel the love of God!

It was during this time that she had an occasion to leave her spiritual director who had guided her so thoroughly in the grace of God, and to submit herself to another more renowned spiritual director, but one who had no grace from God to guide her soul. He took her off of frequent Communion, and she began to give herself up to distractions and the world. Soon, she gave up the practice of meditation which had conquered her many passions in the past. This proved extremely harmful to her soul, and finding she was miserable in the midst of her infidelities to God, plagued by her conscience, she decided to have recourse to Mary to whom she had been consecrated and, '. . . whom no one ever invokes in vain.'

After making a novena and participating in a retreat, Perrine knelt before an altar of our Lady to pray and burned a candle in petition. Soon she felt her heart transformed and her spiritual life changed, and she knew she must return to her former spiritual director. He did indeed receive her back with great charity just as the father of the Prodigal Son had welcomed his lost son home, and she soon began to experience a longing for the religious life.

Faithful to her confessor's guidance, Perrine prepared herself well for her future vocation following after the example of St. Teresa of Avila and found her heart hungrier for the life of a Carmelite nun. The virtues she strove to acquire were mortification, prayer, humility, obedience and charity, all of which the Lord gave her the grace to obtain. Yet, it would be five more years, at the age of 23, before she would leave for the Carmelite monastery in Tours, France.

Perrine, named Sr. Marie de St. Pierre (of St. Peter) and of the Holy Family in religious life, entered Carmel in Tours on November 13, 1839, and shortly after her Holy Profession in 1843 she began to receive a number of communications from Jesus asking her to make known His wish that reparation in the form of devotion to His Holy Face be given a place in the Church.

Communicating himself to her soul, Jesus told her how He grieves seeing that everywhere His Name is blasphemed, and how "**. . . even children blaspheme!**", and how this atrocious sin wounds His Divine Heart, more painfully than other sins. Through blasphemy, the sinner curses Jesus to His Face, attacks Him openly, destroying His Redemption and pronounces his own judgement and condemnation upon himself.

Then Jesus let Sister Marie know that blasphemy was like a poisoned arrow which continually wounded His Heart, and that He wished to give to her a "Golden Arrow" to wound Him deliciously and which would heal the malicious wounds which sinners cause Him. He taught her to say the Golden Arrow prayer as a means to make reparation for the sin of blasphemy and as a preparation for the great 'Reparatory Work' which He would start through her.

Christ also protested of how the holy day of Sunday was being profaned and complained about the blows against the Church and religious worship by secret societies. It was then that He revealed to her the mystery of the reparatory work of His Holy Face, and the pious office which Veronica had rendered to Him in wiping His Face covered with dust, sweat, and blood; outrages which the impious renewed by their blasphemies.

Jesus said to her in 1845:

> I seek Veronicas to wipe and honor My Divine Face, which has few adorers. Who wishes to console Me? Who desires to love Me? For you, I give you My Face, with the aim of recompensing you for the great desires your heart has conceived. I give it to you in the Name of the Father, by virtue of the Holy Spirit, in the presence

> of the Angels and Saints. I make you the gift of it,
> by the hands of My Most Holy Mother, and
> by Saint Veronica, who will teach you to honor it.
> Through My Holy Face you will work miracles.
>
> According to the care which you will have to
> repair My Portrait, disfigured by blasphemies,
> I will have care of yours, marred by sin. I will
> imprint My Image anew and will make it as beautiful
> as it was when coming from the Baptismal font.

Jesus asks for generous souls to make reparation for the sins of the guilty and to implore God's mercy on all sinners. To give more power to their sacrifices and prayers, He wishes that all these "Veronicas" be united.

> I have still My rod in My Hand, the rod of My
> Justice, if one desires to tear it away, let one put
> the Work of Reparation in its place.

Sister Marie de St. Pierre, in obedience to her Superiors and Bishop, could not launch the Work of Reparation herself, and she suffered greatly as it seemed every time she strove to make advances, she was prevented from promoting the Lord's desires.

> *Monseigneur did not want to decide in favor of the Work, and*
> *his prudence prevented him from taking the initiative. I see*
> *clearly that there is no hope except in the intervention of*
> *Mary, our powerful advocate; and I recite the Rosary every*
> *day to obtain the salvation of France and the establishment of*
> *the Work of Reparation in all the towns of the Kingdom. All*
> *my prayers, my Communions, my desires, and all my thoughts*
> *were directed toward this Work, so dear to my heart. If it had*
> *been possible for me, I would have liked to proclaim it all over*
> *France, making known to my homeland, the dangers which*
> *were threatening it. Ah, how I suffer at being the only witness*
> *of such an important matter and that I am obliged to keep it in*

*the silence of the cloister. Holy Virgin, appear to someone
in the world, and inform him of that which has been
communicated to me on the subject of France.*

Our Lady heard the prayer of the humble sister, and she appeared on 19th of September 1846, to two poor shepherd children, Maximin and Melanie on a hillside in La Salette, France. It is to these children that the Most Holy Virgin reproaches her people on account of the way they despise God's Commandments by the profanation of Sunday and by the atrocious sins of blasphemy.

Sister Marie de St. Pierre rejoices when she and her Carmelite sisters hear from one of their benefactors and a friend to Carmel, Monsieur Leo Dupont, of the Blessed Virgin Mary's visit and messages at La Salette, and she realized that soon the Work of Reparation would be revealed to the world. In March 1847, Jesus said to her:

> **Rejoice, My daughter, the hour is approaching for
> the birth of the Most Beautiful Work that may be under
> Heaven. Offer My heart to My Father, in order to obtain it.**

Sister Marie's Prioress, Mother Mary of the Incarnation, truly believed her little daughter of Carmel, too, and transmitted the information to the Archbishop of Tours, Mgr. Morlot, who also saw the hand of God in the messages to the good nun. But in his timidity, he hesitated to establish the Work of Reparation in his diocese, but he did permit the prayers of Reparation to be printed and disseminated throughout France without Sr. Marie's name attached to them.

One of these pamphlets reached the Bishop of Longres, who himself was pre-occupied with the idea of Reparation, and by June 28th, 1847, the Reparatory Confraternity against blasphemy and the profanation of Sunday was established in a church of St. Dizier. Then on July 30th, a Pontifical Brief raised the Association of Saint Denis to the title of Archconfraternity. Pope Pius IX, then reigning, said that: "The Reparation is a Work destined to save society." He inscribed himself as the head of the register along with seven of his cardinals.

Sr. Marie de St. Pierre had fought the hard battle, and the work of Reparation had begun. But this association was not fully the Work of Reparation which Jesus had asked her for, for it did not deal with reparation by virtue of the Holy Face of Jesus and was not in the diocese of Saint Martin.

On the November 11, 1847, the Feast of St. Martin, Sr. Marie de St. Pierre found herself burdened with more struggle as Jesus asks her to make more appeals to the Archbishop, Mgr. Morlot.

On March 3rd, Jesus communicated to her a final ultimatum in the form of a positive command, that the Ordinary of the Tours diocese or his Secretary, come without delay to the Carmelite convent where she would tell them herself what had been revealed to her the past four and a half years regarding the Work of Reparation to the Holy Face.

Following the request by the Prioress, the Archbishop sent his secretary to the monastery to speak with Sister Marie de St. Pierre. After listening to her appeal and asking her specific questions, he let her know that the Archbishop's response was not a positive one. He told her while she was allowed to apply herself personally to the Work of Reparation, she was never again to ask for the establishment of the Work in the diocese, and to stop the distributing of the pamphlets. Sister Marie de St. Pierre, the Carmelite monastery, and Monsieur Dupont all submitted themselves to this ecclesiastical authority in obedience and humility.

It all began to come to an end for Sister Marie de St. Pierre on March 30th, 1848, when our Lord tells His little servant:

> Your pilgrimage is advancing. The end of combat
> is approaching. Soon you will see My Face in Heaven.

From that time on, she thought only of Heaven and abandoned herself to the will of God and His desire for her. On Good Friday, at three o'clock, she prostrated herself before her Spouse, face to the ground, and renewed her act of perfect abandonment in the spirit of reparation. She had given all she could, except her very living, breathing life, and that quickly changed not long after her oblation to the Lord.

She had been healthy during her religious life, following all the religious exercises prescribed by the Holy Rule. But very quickly, she became terminally ill with pulmonary tuberculosis, and on top of this, she developed an ulcerated throat which fittingly symbolized her role in life as a victim soul repairing for the sins of blasphemy.

With her inflamed, ulcerated throat, raw and aching 'as if pierced by thorns' she was made unable to address or ask for the Work of Reparation ever again. For almost three months she was unable to eat solid foods, only a small amount of liquids, but all of this she endured and offered up as she prayed for the conversion and salvation of souls.

A little while before she died, she was questioned about the Devotion to the Holy Face:

> I have the greatest hopes. The plans of the wicked will
> be foiled! It was to accomplish this that the Work of
> Reparation to the Holy Face was revealed. Now that this is
> done, my career is ended. It was for this Work that God
> had placed me on earth, as our Lord has made known to me.
> Oh, how true it is that God has means of satisfying His justice
> which are unknown to men.

When asked if she could offer her sufferings for someone's particular intention, she answered:

> I do not know whether I am free to do so because I am entirely
> consecrated as a victim to the cause of the Work of Reparation.

July 7th, she began her death agony, staying conscious until the end. Though her slight body was racked by the disease and already cold, she continued to pray the prayers of reparation and to whisper to the end, "Jesus, Mary, Joseph! Come, Lord Jesus! Sit Nomen Domini benedictum!" May the Name of the Lord be blessed!

Sr. Marie de St. Pierre died in the odor of sanctity on Saturday, July 8th, 1848, just four months after she spoke with the Archbishop's secretary who told her to not ask again for the establishment of the Work of Reparation in the diocese.

A marker in the wall of the Carmel chapel was inscribed with these words:

HERE LIES
SISTER MARIE DE ST. PIERRE
AND OF THE HOLY FAMILY
PROFESSED OF THIS MONASTERY
DIED 8TH JULY 1848
AGED 31 YEARS AND NINE MONTHS
HAVING BEEN IN RELIGION NINE YEARS
AND EIGHT MONTHS

**Lord, Thou wilt hide me in
the secret of Thy Face**

O God, our Protector, behold us, and cast
Your eyes upon the Face of Your Christ.
(Ps. LXXXIII, 9)

THE REVELATIONS
to
Sister Mary of Saint Peter

The following excerpts are from the book, *Life of Sister Mary de St. Pierre, Carmelite of Tours*, an autobiography composed from her letters kept in the monastery, compiled and edited by L'Abbe Janvier (1884), a Priest of the Holy Face. It was translated from the authentic French manuscripts which, also came directly from the archives of the Monastery of Discalced Carmelites, at Tours, France, where Sister lived and died:

> *One day Our Lord made me understand that I must obey my Superiors rather than any communication which I believed that He Himself had given me.*
>
> *Our Lord revealed to me that His Work of Reparation was to have as its aim not only reparation for blasphemy, but also reparation for the profanation of the Holy Day of the Lord, both enormous sins, arousing the anger of God...*

If God would have allowed the Archbishop (who had pronounced favorably on her messages) to tell me that all my communications were illusions, then I would have abandoned all, for by the grace of God I always had more confidence in the words of my Superiors than in any interior words which I thought I heard spoken by Our Lord, since in these we may sometimes be mistaken, whereas faith never makes us err. And the Saviour in speaking of Superiors said:

Who hears you, hears Me.

We cannot, therefore, be mistaken in hearing them.

April 26, 1843:

Apply yourself diligently to honor My Sacred Heart and the Heart of My Mother. Never separate these Two Hearts. It is My desire that you pray to these two Hearts for yourself and for sinners. I, in turn, will forget your past faults, and, furthermore, I will grant you even more graces than before.

THE GOLDEN ARROW

August 26, 1843:

My name is everywhere blasphemed! There are even children who blaspheme!

He then made me see that this frightful sin wounds His Divine Heart more grievously than all other sins showing me how by blasphemy the sinner curses Him to His Face, attacks Him publicly, and pronounces His own judgement and condemnation.

Our Lord then made me visualize the act of blasphemy as a 'poisoned arrow' continually wounding His Divine Heart.

After that, He revealed to me that He wanted to give me a 'Golden
Arrow' *which would have the power of wounding Him delightfully,
and which would also heal those other wounds inflicted by sin.*

The following is the formula of the 'Golden **Arrow'** *which
is an* '**Act of Praise'** *that our Lord Himself dictated to me,
notwithstanding my unworthiness, in reparation for blasphemy:*

> May the Most Holy, Most Sacred, Most Adorable,
> Most Incomprehensible, and Unutterable Name of
> God be always praised, blessed, loved, adored, and
> glorified in Heaven, on earth, and under the earth, by
> all the creatures of God, and by the Sacred Heart of
> Our Lord Jesus Christ in the most Holy Sacrament of
> the Altar. Amen.

November 10, 1843: *The Savior insisted that this Novena
(by our community) be made entirely in a spirit of Reparation,
for the outrageous blasphemies of which our nation is guilty and for
the specific intention of obtaining mercy … He urged me to ask that the
prayers of atonement for blasphemies be printed and disseminated …*

November 24, 1843:

> The whole earth is covered with crimes, and the violation
> of the first three of the Ten Commandments of God
> has aroused the anger of My Father. The crimes that
> fill up the cup of wickedness are blasphemies against
> God's Holy Name and the profanation of Sundays.
> These sins have reached to the very throne of Almighty
> God, and they have provoked His wrath, which is
> about to strike everywhere unless His Justice be
> appeased. Never before have these crimes reached
> such a peak …

I desire, and this most urgently, that there be
formed, to honor the name of My Father, an
association, properly approved and well organized.

December 7, 1843: *My soul is terrified at what our Lord has
just made me hear during prayer this morning, charging me with
the duty of transmitting His message to my Superiors without any
fear of being deceived. He said He was incensed with anger against
our nation, and that He has sworn in His wrath to avenge Himself
if Reparation to the honor of His Divine Father were not made for
all the blasphemies of which the people are guilty . . .*

*He then declared that His Mercy was on the verge of giving
way to His Justice, and that His wrath would overflow with a
fury such as had never yet been heard of before.*

*Greatly frightened, I pleaded: "My Lord, permit me to ask
You if You would grant our nation pardon if this Atonement
for which You ask were made to God?*

Our Lord answered me:

Yes, I will grant it pardon once more, but mark
My word, once! And since this crime of blasphemy
extends over the WHOLE nation, and since it is
PUBLIC, I demand that Reparation be extended
to ALL THE CITIES of the nation, and that it be
PUBLIC. Woe to those cities that will not make
this Reparation!

NO ONE TO CONSOLE ME

February 2, 1844: *Our Savior desires that this Association
be placed under the patronage of St. Michael, St. Martin,
and St. Louis asking that each member should daily say one
Our Father, one Hail Mary, and one Glory Be together with
the Act of Praise called the Golden Arrow.*

*Our Lord told me that He desired each member to wear
a special cross and that on one side should be engraved the
words* 'Blessed be the Name of God,' *and on the reverse
side the words:* 'Begone Satan!' *To all those wearing this
Holy Cross, our Lord promised a special resourcefulness
to conquer the demon of blasphemy, adding that every time
one hears a curse, he should repeat the two short inscriptions,
and he will thus overcome the evil one and render glory to God.*

February 25, 1844: *Our Lord made known to me that only Reparation
could disarm the Justice of God, because the guilt of men had provoked
His anger. He made me understand that His Sacred Heart desires, through
this means, to bestow mercy on mankind. Divine Jesus addressed all with
these words:*

> Oh, you, who are My friends and faithful children,
> look and see if there be any sorrow like Mine.
> Everywhere My enemies despise and insult both
> My Eternal Father and My Church, the cherished
> spouse of My Heart. Will no one rise up to console
> Me by defending the glory of My Father, and the
> honor of My Spouse which has been so cruelly
> attacked? I can no longer remain in the midst of a
> people that will continue to be so heedless and so
> ungrateful. Look at the torrent of the tears that stream
> from My eyes! Can I find no one to wipe away these
> tears by making reparation to My Father, and
> imploring forgiveness for the guilty?

March 16, 1844:

> You cannot comprehend the malice and abomination
> of this sin of blasphemy. If My Justice were not
> restrained by My Mercy, indeed, it would instantly
> crush the guilty. In fact, all creatures, even those that
> are inanimate, (including the elements of nature),
> would avenge this outrage against their Creator's
> majesty, but I have an eternity in which to punish

the guilty . . .

Oh, if you only knew what great merit you acquire
by saying even once, *'Admirable is the Name of God'*,
in the spirit of reparation for blasphemy!

For your badge I give you the cross and thorns
that lay buried within My Heart. Do not turn away
from this cross nor from these thorns, because My
daughter, you are being called to a high perfection.
Think only of Me, and in return I will think of you.
Attend to My affairs, and I promise you that I will
take care of yours . . .

I SEEK VERONICAS

October 11, 1845: *Our Lord vividly showed me the pious deed of
charity which St. Veronica performed towards Him when, with
her veil, she wiped His Most Holy Face covered with spittle, dust,
sweat, and blood. Then this Divine Savior told me that in our present
age the wicked, by their blasphemies, renew all those outrages that
disfigured His Holy Face on that occasion . . .*

*Following this, our Lord told me that by practicing Reparation for
blasphemy, we render Him the same service as did the pious Veronica,
and that just as He looked with kindly eyes upon this holy woman during
His Passion, so would He regard with affection all those who make reparation.
I could see from our Lord's attitude that He had a very tender love for
St. Veronica.*

October 27, 1845: *I understand that as the Sacred Heart of Jesus is
the exterior object offered for our adoration to represent His boundless
love in the Most Holy Sacrament of Altar, so, in a parallel manner, the
Face of Jesus is the exterior object offered for the adoration of the
members in the Work of Reparation . . .*

By virtue of this Holy Face, offered to the Eternal Father, we can appease His just anger and obtain the conversion of the wicked and of blasphemers … I saw that the impious, in uttering wicked words and in blaspheming the Holy Name of God, spit in our Lord's Face and cover it with mud.

I comprehend, too, that all the blows which dissenters inflict upon Holy Church, attacking religion, are a renewal of the numerous blows which our Lord's face received in the Passion, and that these blows were inflicted on Him by those who attempted to stamp out the Works and Words of God.

After this vision, our Lord said to me **'I seek Veronicas to wipe and venerate My Divine Face, which has but few adorers!'** *And then He assured me that all persons who would apply themselves to this Work of Reparation would perform the same service in His behalf as she did.*

October 28, 1845: *Our Lord invited me to kiss most lovingly the Image of His Holy Face in a spirit of reparation.*

January 5, 1846: *The Divine Saviour warned me that I would have much to suffer because the herd of blasphemers was in a special manner under the prince of demons, that is Lucifer himself. As for the various flocks composed of other sinners, for example the immoral, the drunkards, and the avaricious, Lucifer left these sinners to be led by the other less powerful demons … but that blasphemers are Lucifer's own particular herd.* (This is even more relevant now in the 21st century with the rise of Satanism, black masses, witchcraft, desecration of Catholic churches, blasphemies, etc.)

Our Saviour told me that He had great plans of showing mercy to this particular class of sinner … through the inauguration of the Work of Reparation.

SOME PROMISES

March 12, 1846: *Our Lord revealed Himself to me this morning after Holy Communion, and He made known to me that two persons had rendered Him a particular service during His Passion. The first of these was the pious Veronica who honored His Sacred Humanity by wiping His Adorable Face on the road to Calvary. The second person was the Good Thief, who from the cross as from a pulpit, openly defended the Saviour's cause, confessing His Divinity, and glorifying Him while He was being blasphemed by the other thief and by the mob.*

Our Lord made me understand that these two persons were presented to the members of the Association of Reparation as models. St. Veronica is the model for persons of her own sex who are called to serve Him, not by preaching sermons, but by wiping His Holy Face in a spirit of reparation for blasphemies through their prayers, their praises and adoration.

The Good Thief, however, who so openly and boldly defended the Saviour's cause on Calvary, is held up more especially as a model to priests who must now imitate him, and through their public preaching, defend the cause of Reparation.

After telling me this, our Saviour invited me to notice what magnificent rewards He had immediately bestowed on these two persons for their services in His behalf. To the first, that is to St. Veronica, He gave a picture of Himself by impressing the divine features of His Sacred Face on her veil. As for the other, that is the Good Thief (St. Dismas), our Lord conferred upon him, that very day, the gift of eternal blessedness by admitting him into the Kingdom of Heaven.

Then our Lord promised me that all who defended His cause in the Work of Reparation, whether by their words, their prayers, or by their writing, He would Himself defend before His Eternal Father, and that He would give them His Kingdom. Then it seemed to me that

*our Lord urged me to extend this promise in His Name to His priests,
who through a crusade of preaching, would advance the cause of Reparation.*

*As for His spouses who would strive to honor and wipe His Holy Face in a
spirit of atoning for blasphemies, our Lord promised that at death He
would purify the face of their souls by effacing the stains of sin, and
that He would restore them to their original beauty. Jesus said:*

> Write down these promises for they will make a
> greater impression on souls than all that you have
> already said regarding this Work, because these
> promises which speak of eternal rewards, will
> greatly stimulate the interest of the faithful, which
> interest I do not condemn since I have given My life to
> merit the Kingdom of Heaven for sinners. You will be
> guilty of an act of injustice if you do not make know
> these revelations!

> Those who embrace this work of Reparation with
> true piety will not be lost, for I myself will defend
> them before My Father, and I will give them the
> Kingdom Heaven. I will grant them the grace of
> final perseverance . . .

> According to the care you take in making reparation to
> My Face disfigured by blasphemies, so will I take care
> of yours which has been disfigured by sin. I will
> reprint therein My image, and render it as beautiful as it
> was on leaving the Baptismal font . . .

> Do not be astonished at these promises which I make
> in favor of those who devote themselves to repairing
> for blasphemies against God's Holy Name through
> the devotion to My Sacred Face, because this Work
> of Reparation is the very essence of Charity, and those
> who possess Charity, possess life.

SAVE SOULS FROM HELL

November 22, 1846:

> My daughter, I take you today for my stewardess. I place
> My Holy Face in your hands, that you may offer
> it unceasingly to My Father for the salvation of your
> country.
>
> Turn this Divine gift to good profit, for the treasure of
> My Holy Face, in itself, possesses such tremendous value
> that through it all the affairs of My household and
> readily be settled. Through this Holy Face you will
> obtain the conversion of sinners. Nothing that you ask
> in virtue of the Holy Face will be refused you. Oh, if you
> only knew how pleasing is the sight of My Face to
> My Father.

December 21, 1846: *Our Lord showed me the multitude of souls
that were continually falling into hell, and He invite me in a most
touching manner to help these poor sinners. He pointed out to me that
Religious in particular have a most strict obligation towards these poor,
blind souls who precipitate themselves into the eternal abyss; and that
if other charitable souls would ask grace and mercy for these blinded ones,
God's mercifulness would open their eyes. Our Lord said:*

> My daughter, I give you My Face and My Heart. I give
> you My Blood, and I open to you My Wounds. Draw
> from these and pour out their spiritual treasures on
> others. Buy without money. My Blood is the price for
> souls! Oh, how painful it is to My Heart to see
> remedies, which have cost Me so dearly, scorned! Ask
> of My Father as many souls as was the number of drops
> of Blood that I shed in My Passion!

*On another day, Our Lord showed me His Holy Cross, saying
that He had given birth to all His children on this bed of pain.*

Then He made me understand that in carrying my cross for
Love of Him, and through prayers, I would obtain eternal life
for those who are dead to grace, and whose resurrection he
desired so ardently. Oh, what yearnings I see in the Heart of
Jesus for the salvation of sinners!

NOTHING YOU ASK IN VIRTUE
OF THE HOLY FACE WILL BE REFUSED YOU

January 10th, 1847: *Our Lord told me that, in imitation of Him,*
I shall spend my remaining years pursuing His sheep that
are lost. Oh, blindness of men that runs after the perishable
riches of earth, whose aggregate value could not purchase
even a single soul! Yet, in the meantime it scorns all
that our Redeemer has done for us, which treasure suffices
to purchase millions of souls, if we but present His merits
at the bank of Divine Mercy.

March 2, 1847: *I contemplated Jesus surrounded with great*
majesty and splendor, but He said:

> My daughter, I prefer that you consider Me covered
> with wounds, because sinners continually inflict them
> upon Me . . . I am not known, I am not loved, and
> My Commandments are scorned.
>
> Sinners are snatched from this world, and they are
> swept into Hell like the dust is carried away by the fury
> of a tornado. Have pity on your brothers and pray for
> them! With the veil of your tender love, wipe the
> Blood which flows from My Wounds. Love me . . . and
> when you raise your heart to Me in love, I will accept it
> from you and keep it in security.

Make Reparation

MORE WARNINGS

January 26, 1846: *The following are the terrifying words which our Lord spoke to me:*

> The face of this nation has become unsightly in the eyes of my Father. The people are provoking the arm of His Justice. To obtain mercy, offer, therefore, to the Eternal Father the Face of His Son, in which He takes His delights. Unless this be done, the nation will experience God's just punishments. Yes, the country's deliverance from these evils lies in the Face of the Saviour. Behold here another proof of My Goodness towards this nation which repays Me with ingratitude!

October 4, 1846:

> My Justice is irritated on account of the profanations of the Holy day of Sunday. I seek a victim . . .

Our Lord commanded me to receive Holy Communion every Sunday for these three particular intentions:

1ˢᵗ. In a spirit of atoning for all forbidden works done on Sundays, which as Holy days are to be sanctified.

2ⁿᵈ. To appease Divine Justice, which was on the very verge of striking on account of the profanation of Holy days.

3ʳᵈ. To implore the conversion of those sinners who desecrate Sundays, and to succeed in obtaining the cessation of forbidden Sunday labor. Jesus invited me to offer His Holy Face to His Eternal Father, as a means of obtaining these gifts of Mercy.

Soon I received proof that it was indeed He who foretold to me what chastisements of God's Justice would be felt because of the profanation of Sunday. There occurred so frightful and so unprecedented an overflowing of the River Loire as had not been seen in centuries. The whole city of Tours was in imminent danger, as terror and confusion gripped the citizens.

Everywhere people acknowledged that an Omnipotent hand was wielding the elements at will, and even those persons who professed hardly any religious belief whatsoever, now openly admitted that it was only through a miracle that the whole city of Tours did not perish. But the real cause that provoked God to send this punishment on the city was the profanation of Sunday, as Our Lord Himself told me, yet this principal fact continues to be ignored. But what filled my soul with sadness was an interior light which Our Lord granted me, by which I saw that God's justice was preparing to send still other chastisements. Our Lord communicated to me that this time He would use as instruments of punishment, not the elements of nature, but **'the malice of revolutionary men'.**

On September 18, 1846, our Lady appeared to two little children on a mountain in La Salette, France. She gave an almost identical message of warning, saying:

> *'Six days I have given you to labor, the seventh I have kept for myself, and you will not give it to me. Those who drive the carts cannot swear without introducing the name of my Son. These are the two things which make the arm of my Son so heavy.'*

Our Lady then foretold great punishment, particularly in the form of famine and disease that would befall the people if they did not amend their ways. History records the dreadful fulfillment of her predictions because the people would not listen. (Is not the same happening in our day concerning the message from Our Lady of Fatima?)

> *'Those who drive the carts cannot swear without introducing the name of my Son ... '*
> *Our Lady of LaSalette*

October 25, 1846: *After Holy Communion, our Lord told me that the cup of Divine Justice had been only partly poured out upon us, and I was then shown still other punishments to come...*
It was not long before we realized the truth of this communication. Soon after this, the city of Tours shook with the shocking news of a Conspiracy by the Communists to seize the city government and make themselves its masters. Providentially, the bloody project of these revolutionary men was discovered in time, and although the people of the whole city were in imminent danger, they escaped unharmed. Without Our Lord's help, we would have all been lost.

March 14th, 1847: *Our Lord showed me the sins of blasphemy and profanation of Sunday under the symbol of two pumps with which men, guilty of these crimes, are drawing the waters of God's wrath on our country and which is in danger of being submerged if the Work of Reparation, which He has given us in His Mercy as a means of deliverance, be not established. He told me that the Society known as the Communists had so far made only one outbreak, but that they were working secretly to advance their schemes, saying:*

> Oh, if you only knew their secret and diabolical plots and their anti-Christian principles! They are waiting for a favorable day in order to inflame the whole country. To obtain mercy, ask that this Work of Reparation be established . . .

March 29, 1847:

> My daughter, I have a great love for obedience. Submit to them, therefore, so that seeing you always so obedient to your Superiors in everything that I communicate to you, they will be able to recognize the spirit by which you are being led. Nevertheless, it is My Will that these revelations, which I have given you, be made known to your highest superior (the Archbishop).

March 29, 1847: *Our Lord commanded me to make war on the Communists because He said they were the enemies of the Church and Her Christ. He told me that most of these wolfish men who are now Communists, had been born into the Church, whose bitter enemies they now openly declare themselves to be. Then our Saviour added:*

> I have already told you that I hold you in My hands as an arrow. I now want to hurl this arrow against My enemies. To arm you for the battle ahead, I give you the weapons of My Passion - that is My Cross which these enemies dread, and the other instruments of my tortures. Go forward to meet these foes with the alertness of a child, and the bravery of a courageous soldier. Receive for this mission the benediction of the Father, of the Son, and of the Holy Ghost . . . The weapons of My enemies inflict death, but My weapons give life.

April 1, 1847: *Our Lord continues still to charge me with the mission of making war on the Communists. He supplies me with grace and the light for the battle. The instruments of His Passion serve me as weapons of war, while the Holy Name of God, which is so terrifying to the demons, as also that of the Blessed Virgin Mary, serve me as ammunition. To further rouse me to this battle against God's enemies, whom I understand through a special light to be, indeed formidable, our Lord said:*

> When a soldier knows that the reason for the war to which he is called to fight is an injury against his ruler, he burns with indignation to avenge this insult and therefore, arms himself fearlessly for the encounter. Think now, My daughter, of the outrages inflicted on Me by this society of Communists. They are the ones who have dragged Me from My tabernacles and desecrated My sanctuaries. These Communists have also dared to lay their hands on the priests of the Lord, but all their plotting is in vain, because their schemes will not succeed . . .

This information must not remain fruitless in you, because I am giving you these facts in order to fire you with new enthusiasm to carry on the fight. Act in a spirit of simplicity, because if you will indulge in too much human reasoning, you will not be an adequate tool in My hands. (In other words, as our Lady requested at Fatima, fight with the weapons of prayer, penance, and reparation given by the Lord, rather than fighting the enemy with his own weapons of hate, confusion, and division on his own terms, and thus lose effectiveness.)

December 2nd 1847:

> The executioners crucified Me on Friday,
> but Christians crucify Me on Sunday.

THE STORM BREAKS

February 13, 1847: *Our Lord made known to me that terrible woes were impending, and He said:*

> Pray, pray for the Church is
> threatened by a fearful tempest!

The Saviour made me understand that His Justice was greatly irritated by mankind for its sins, but particularly for those that directly outrage the Majesty of God – that is, Communism, atheism, cursing, and the desecration of Sundays.

February 20, 1847: *It was made known to my soul by an interior light that the crisis was at hand. I heard these words:* 'The Lord has strung His bow, and He is about to discharge His arrows!'

I comprehended that this scandal, if I may so express myself, must of necessity come to pass. For more than four years had the arm of the Lord been raised over our guilty heads. Almost immediately following this communication from our Lord, news of a serious revolution in Paris shook the very foundations of the French government and all of Europe. King Louis Philippe, who after 18 years felt himself securely established as monarch of France, was forced to flee with his family into exile . . .

The Lord told me that in consequence of the initial efforts to establish somewhat the Work of Reparation, our country, which was to be almost entirely destroyed by the darts of His Justice, would now only be partly punished by the terrible flames of His anger. Oh, how I long to entreat all the Bishops to establish the Work of Reparation in their dioceses.

CHURCH APPROVAL

After her death, in 1848, Reparation and Devotion of the Most Holy Face of Jesus was kept up chiefly through the efforts and fervor of a retired lawyer of Tours, a devoted friend of the nun. Leo Dupont, having obtained a picture of the Holy Face, which was touched to the true relic of the veil of Veronica at the Vatican, hung it prominently in his home. Many extraordinary favors were granted those who came to his home to pray before the picture. Three months after his death, his shrine home was transformed into a public chapel by the Archbishop. Soon afterwards, Pope Leo XIII approved the devotion to the Holy Face of Jesus through the formality of a Papal Brief.

So was erected in perpetuity, the Archconfraternity of Reparation in the Oratory of Leo Dupont, in 1885. There, to this day, priests still carry on the mission of Sister Marie de St. Pierre, to whom Our Lord revealed over 100 years ago the real weapon that is destined to overthrow Communism.

That weapon is the devotion to the Holy Face of Jesus, as a means of Reparation for the outrageous crimes of modern freethinkers, atheists, blasphemers, (Satanists), and the profaners of the Lord's Day. These are the evils that more than any other cry to Heaven for vengeance and that today bring us face to face with the threat of nuclear war, whose consequence would admittedly be the destruction of all civilization as we know it.

THE LITTLE VERONICAS
Story by Donna Sue Berry
Illustrations by Jane Frances Privett

The bell had just rung for religion class to begin at Our Lady of the Rosary Catholic school for girls, and while the students settled down into their seats, Sister Mary Theresa stood in front of them with a smile on her face. "Can any of you tell me what the Sixth Station of the Cross is?" she asked.

Immediately, Tricia and Kitten's hands flew up into the air, waving them around, both anxious to answer Sister's question. Rose and Sue, two of the shyer girls in class, slowly raised their hands as well. In the back of the classroom, Nancy and Cathy were too busy whispering to each other to hear Sister's question, but Gloria shushed them both while stretching her own hand up as high as she could in the hopes that Sister would call on her.

"Gloria." Sister had chosen.

"It's where Veronica wiped the Face of Jesus!" She responded very sure of herself.

Cindy, who hadn't raised her hand, eagerly blurted out, "Jesus was carrying his cross on the road to Calvary and . . ." But before she could finish, Debra almost shouted, "He was going up to Calvary to be crucified and he was wearing a crown of thorns on his head!"

Sister Theresa nodded, looking at her very enthusiastic students. "Just a moment, girls," she said, "Let's hear what Sue and Rose have to say, too."

Sue responded, "Jesus had been scourged, and so he was in a lot of pain."

"But Sue," Rose said looking at her friend, "before they scourged him, he had prayed so hard in the Garden of Gethsemane that he sweated drops of blood!"

"Sister," Tricia asked hurriedly, eager to be a part of the discussion, "isn't it true that Jesus could see all the sins of the world, and didn't he know that he would suffer and die for all of us, and because of his sacrifice, weren't the gates of heaven opened again?"

Kitten, answered Tricia not waiting for Sr. Mary Theresa's response. "Well of course he could see and know all of that, Tricia, but he also saw all the souls who would not be saved because they would rather stay in sin, and that caused him greater pain!"

"He must have been really sad," said Nancy thoughtfully, "to know that he would suffer for so many people who would not go to heaven."

Cathy asked a question. "Sister, who was St. Veronica?"

"St. Veronica", sister answered, "was a woman who was there in Jerusalem the day that Jesus was crucified. While he was carrying his heavy, wooden cross to Calvary, Veronica saw him fall and could see the horrible pain that he was in. She saw his face which was covered with blood, sweat, dirt, and spit from the mean Roman soldiers who were forcing him along the way.

At just the right moment, Veronica pushed her way through the crowd of people who were following Jesus and past the group of soldiers surrounding him as he lay on the ground under the cross. She was able to get right up next to him, and she quickly pulled the veil from off her head and placed it against his face to wipe it."

"Girls," Sr. Mary Theresa continued, "can you only imagine Veronica's love and compassion for Jesus as she knelt down next to him, and how they must have looked into each other's eyes?" Sister was silent for a few seconds to let the image of her words sink into the girls' thoughts.

"I imagine that it didn't take long" she said, "for the soldiers to pull Veronica away from Jesus so that they could force him back up and toward the hill where they would crucify him. When Veronica was finally alone and able to look at the veil, she saw that he had left her a gift. On the veil was the image of his face! A picture of himself for her to treasure!"

"Wow!" said Cindy under her breath. "That's unreal" murmured some of the other girls.

"To this day," Sr. Mary Theresa said "The veil that Veronica used to wipe the face of Jesus is kept at the Vatican in Rome, in St. Peter's Cathedral, and every 5th Sunday of Lent the Vatican displays the relic for all to see. Many copies of Veronica's Veil have been made over the centuries with the Vatican's stamp of approval and given to people around the world."

About that time, the classroom door opened and in walked Sr. Margaret Mary with what looked like a big framed picture covered with cloth. "Good morning, girls", she said. "Good morning, Sister" they replied.

"Class, Sr. Margaret Mary has brought you an authentic copy of Veronica's Veil to look at." And with that, Sr. Mary Theresa pulled the wrapping off the picture.

Tears immediately sprang into Cathy and Rose's eyes, and Sue grabbed a tissue as they all looked at the copy of the image of Christ's face on Veronica's Veil.

The room was silent for a few seconds, and then Sister Margaret Mary asked the girls if they knew how they could be like St. Veronica and wipe the Face of Jesus every day. The students shook their heads and responded, "No, Sister."

"Well, over the centuries" she said "there have been many saints who were devoted to the Holy Face of Jesus. Saints such as St. Gertrude and St. Mechtilde. But in 1843, Jesus appeared to Sister Mary of St. Peter, a young Carmelite nun in a monastery in the city of Tours, France. He told her that when people blaspheme by cursing and saying the name of God in vain, that it is just as if the Roman soldiers wounded Jesus all over again.

Jesus told Sr. Mary of St. Peter *"I seek Veronicas to wipe my face. "*

He said he wanted her to pray and offer up her sacrifices to repair for the sins of blasphemy that are committed against the most Holy Name of God every day throughout the world.

Sister Mary of St. Peter then received a prayer from Jesus called the 'Golden Arrow', and he told her that every time she would pray it, it would be like a golden arrow wounding his heart delightfully. This prayer would repair, or make-up for, so many sins of blasphemy committed against God, and this is called 'making reparation'. He said that each time she would say this prayer that she would become like St. Veronica wiping his bruised and bloody face.

Sister Mary Theresa looked very thoughtfully at her students and spoke. "Girls, would you like to become like St. Veronica?"

"How can we do that?", asked Mary Ann, the quietest girl in the class.

"By placing a picture of the Holy Face of Jesus in your home and by saying the Golden Arrow prayer." said Sr. Mary Theresa. "Would you like to say the Golden Arrow prayer with me right now?"

"Oh, yes, Sister!" They all agreed, and kneeling in front of the Holy Face picture, they bowed their heads, made the Sign of the Cross, and prayed:

May the most holy, the most sacred, most adorable, most incomprehensible, and unutterable Name of God, be forever praised, blessed, loved, adored and glorified, in heaven, on earth, and under the earth, by all the creatures of God, and by the Sacred Heart of Our Lord Jesus Christ in the Most Holy Sacrament of the altar. Amen.

Sr. Mary Theresa smiled knowingly at Sr. Margaret Mary as her students recited the Golden Arrow prayer. By saying this prayer her girls had made an act of reparation for blasphemy, and they had lovingly wiped the Face of Jesus.

They had become Little Veronicas.

The Holy Man of Tours,
Venerable Leo Dupont
(January 24th, 1797 - March 18th, 1876)

Before her holy death, Sister Marie de St. Pierre had said that her mission was ended, but where she finished her task, Monsieur Leo Dupont moved forward in their one and same desire to make known the Work of Reparation in the Devotion to the Holy Face. He would revere her memory and continue to foster her ideas and desire for reparation while her writings were still under Episcopal seal.

However, he didn't have long to wait before he received supernatural help from Heaven. Something miraculous happened at the Vatican that would validate his endeavor to continue to propagate Sister Marie's mandate and to establish the Work of Reparation on earth. Leo Dupont recorded the miracle in his letters:

"In the month of January 1849, during the exile of Pius IX at
Gaeta, public prayers, by order of the Sovereign Pontiff,
were offered in all the churches to implore the Mercy of the
All Powerful on the Pontifical State. On this occasion, the
Wood of the True Cross and the Veil of Veronica were exposed
at St. Peter's in the Vatican. Now on this veil, one can scarcely
distinguish any more the sacred features of Our Lord,
JESUS CHRIST. On the 6th of January, Feast of the Epiphany,
the Holy Face, which is on Veronica's veil, appeared distinctly,
even through the silk which covers it, and which completely
prevents one from distinguishing the features. Then, on the
third day of the Exposition, the Veil itself became colored and
the Face of Our Saviour appeared as if living, in the midst
of a gentle light. The Divine Face showed itself in relief, with
an ashy pale color, and the eyes sunken and animated
with the expression of profound severity.

The Canons who were on guard near the Holy Relic
immediately notified the clergy of the Basilica, M.M. the
Canons Lucidi, Castagneti, and San Pierri. The great bells
were sounded, and the people hastened. The Holy Face
remained fully alive for three hours, before an immense
crowd. The most inexplicable impression was upon every
face; many were weeping, and all were struck by the miracle.
A notary apostolic was called to record the event, and a copy
of this was sent to the Holy Father in Gaeta. For several days,
no one at Rome spoke of anything else except this astonishing
prodigy. In the evening, several white veils on which the
Holy Face was represented, were touched to the miraculous
veil. These veils had to be sent to France.

Towards the end of last Lent, some came to us in Tours,
through the Benedictines of Arras. The Mother Prioress
of Carmel had the goodness to give me two copies. I placed
one in the chapel of M. Redon at the Lazarists (where
Leo Dupont had founded the Nocturnal Adoration for men),
and I kept the other one. I placed this Holy Face in my
drawing room, on the left side of the chimney piece, in the
cavity above a little cupboard which would be suitable to

receive a lamp. It was Holy Wednesday. Hardly had it been placed there when I was suddenly struck by a feeling which came from the depth of my heart. I said to myself: 'Can this image of the Divine Face of the Saviour of men be exposed in a Christian's home during the great week of the Passion without an extra sign of respect, adoration and love being given to it? No certainly, it will not be like this'. And this is how I had the idea of lighting this lamp before the Holy Face, with the intention of only letting it burn during the rest of Holy Week. I immediately carried out this project."

Leo lit the lamp and then immediately knelt before the image to honor Christ – Jesus, whose greatest agony was His mental pain, which shown in the details of the image of His Holy Face through Veronica's veil.

When explaining the reason later for the lamp burning before the image, Leo said: "I burn the lamp to teach those who enter here that when their business is complete, they must either speak of God or leave." Leo placed a hand-written card on his desk so that visitors would see the instruction. It worked very well, and many times he was able to share with them the Holy Face story.

Not long after he had placed the image with the lamp burning before it, Miss Estell, an acquaintance of Leo's, came to transact some business. While she sat at his desk, she continually rubbed her aching eyes, and having noticed her pain, Leo suggested she go before the Holy Face to pray for relief. A little while later, he knelt beside her, joined her in prayer, and then suggested she rub some of the oil from the lamp upon her eyes. Immediately after she applied the oil, she exclaimed, 'My eyes no longer hurt me!' She felt no pain at all, and the cure was instantaneous! From that moment on, Leo made the decision to keep the lamp burning day and night, and his own devotion to the Holy Face grew even deeper.

Blessed be God
Blessed be His Holy Name!

About a week after Miss Estelle's cure, Leo was visited again, this time by a young man who was limping with a leg injury. Leo anointed his leg and then knelt with him to pray before the image. Again, there was an instantaneous cure, and the young man ran outside jumping and shouting that he had been healed!

He continued to have the sick and lame drop by his home whom he would pray with, instruct, and give encouragement to, and it wasn't long before Monsieur Dupont's reputation also earned him the title of the Holy Man of Tours.

Some weeks after the miraculous cures began, Leo visited the Carmelite convent to let Mother Prioress know about all the cures that had been taking place before the image of the Holy Face. Mother Prioress was impressed!

'Cures through the Holy Face?' She asked.

'Yes', he replied. 'Cures through the Holy Face. It
Seems our Lord is anxious to prove to us the power
of the Devotion to the Holy Face so, He is granting us
miraculous cures. Maybe in due time, after witnessing
these wonderful cures of the body, men will come to
understand the deeper meaning behind this Devotion to
the Holy Face. It may be that they will come to grasp this
before it is too late, before revolutionary men succeed in
robbing them of their dignity, before Communists close up
up their churches and make them slaves of the State. We
have seen enough of this sort of devastation of religion by
now, and unless Reparation is done, unless men come before
the Face of their Saviour to ask His forgiveness and His help,
world revolution will spread, and Communism will enslave
us all!'

'May God forbid this, Mr. Dupont. But as you say, maybe
The miraculous cures will help to prove the truth of Sister
Marie de St. Pierre's revelations of the Holy Face. Maybe the
Archbishop will be impressed with these wonders, and
maybe he will throw open the sealed archives in which

our Sister's revelations are now hidden, And maybe,
just maybe, at last, her life and her mission will become
known to the world!'

As the year ended, he was visited by more and more pilgrims, sometimes numbering as many as 300 persons a day, and many miraculous cures were obtained through the recitation of Litany of the Holy Face (composed by Sister Marie de St. Pierre), the Golden Arrow prayer, and the anointing of the oil from the lamp. Leo began writing an account of the many miracles worked in a journal which soon spilled over into second journal. He filled and gave away small vials of the oil from the lamp that burned before the Holy Face image, which totaled more than eight thousand vials the first year and over sixty thousand vials by the end of the third year. Taking a photograph of the Holy Face image, he had 25,000 lithograph copies made and distributed them to pilgrims, as well.

He received many requests by mail, not only from Europe, but from around the world asking for vials of the Holy Face oil, and all of these he would mail at his own expense to those who asked for it. He received many certificates from reputable physicians recording miraculous cures of their patients. Leo was more than euphoric about the miracles, but more than anything, he desired that the Church authorities, keeping Sister's mission a secret, would approve them and begin the Work of Reparation requested by our Lord to Sister Marie de St. Pierre.

It would be 30 years' worth of prayers, miracles, and Leo's silence about Sr. Marie's revelations from Jesus before a newly appointed archbishop would move swiftly and certainly toward the Work of Reparation. Archbishop Charles Colet released all the writings of and sealed documents concerning the Lord's revelations to Sister Marie, and he had them sent to the learned Benedictine Fathers at the Abbey of Solesmes for their study and quick analysis.

Upon the Abbey returning the documents to the Archbishop with their highest recommendations and approval, Archbishop Colet ordered the life and revelations of Sister Marie de St. Pierre to be published! The Work of Reparation would be approved, and Leo, when he heard the news, was silent for a while, and then spoke, 'Now dost Thou dismiss Thy servant in peace, oh, Lord, for my eyes have seen the salvation of the world!'

He had grown old and ill in his obedience to tirelessly work and privately promote the Devotion to the Holy Face, and he would be able to die in peace knowing that the Church had approved the 'most beautiful work under the sun', the Work of Reparation through the Devotion to the Holy Face.

Leo Dupont died, in the odor of sanctity, on Saturday, March 18th, 1876 at the age of 79.

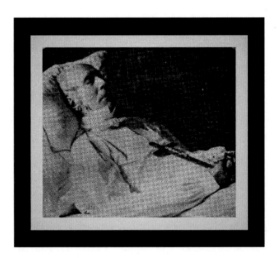

The miracles, continuing even past the death of Leo Dupont, were so numerous, that Pope Blessed Pius IX (1792-1878) declared Leo Dupont to be perhaps one of the greatest miracle workers in Church history!

Shortly after Leo's death, the Archbishop received a proposal from the Carmelite nuns who wanted to purchase Leo's home and keep it a place of pilgrimage to the Holy Face. Their proposal was met with great enthusiasm and quick approval. The house was bought, and the Archbishop took the formal steps to convert the private home and turn Leo's parlor into a public oratory! He had the picture of the Holy Face encased in a new frame of gilt bronze and studded with precious stones, and had it hung over the altar in the new Holy Face Oratory.

Three months after Leo's death, Archbishop Colet, himself, presided over the blessing of the Oratory of the Holy Face and was the first to offer the Holy Sacrifice of the Mass on the new altar. He wove the names of Sister Marie de St. Pierre and Leo Dupont throughout his sermon that day, and he urged those attending to imitate the example of the two Adorers of the Holy Face. He would, from that day forward, disseminate in writing the life and mission of Sister Marie de St. Pierre and her saintly disciple, Leo Dupont. The Cult of the Holy Face would be explained throughout the diocese and the world with the spreading of books and pamphlets that bore the Archbishop's imprimatur.

He immediately appointed a chaplain to attend to the Oratory which saw a spontaneous and overwhelming response to the revelations and the Work of Reparation to the Holy Face. However, the response was too much for the one chaplain, and the archbishop soon formed a diocesan Society of Priests who were to reside in the holy house of Leo Dupont. They became known as the Priests of the Holy Face.

Realizing the importance of the press, Archbishop Colet asked that the Work be explained *in all its details* and even more through the printing of biographies by Father Peter Janvier, who had known Leo personally. In less than five years, Father Janvier had written dual publications of the two adorers of the Holy Face, again, these bearing the Imprimatur of Archbishop Colet. The books were published and translated into English and welcomed by the American Bishops in the United States.

Cardinal Gibbons, of Baltimore, gave the following approbation in writing: 'The Life of the devout Carmelite of Tours is calculated to promote piety and edification not only in cloistered institutions, but also in the ranks of secular life.'

As the Devotion spread across the United States, the main propagator of the Work of Reparation to the Holy Face was the Archbishop of New Orleans, Louisiana, the Most Reverend Napoleon Perche, who, not only gave written approbation to Sister Marie de St. Pierre's mission, but he travelled to Tours, France on a personal visit. A Frenchman himself, and deeply concerned with the affect the devotion was having on France, the Archbishop was so impressed with all that he learned there, that after returning home to New Orleans, he canonically established a Confraternity of Reparation to the Holy Face in his own diocese, choosing the Chapel of the Discalced Carmelite Nuns for devotion. This was the first chapel in the United States entrusted with the Work of Reparation.

Archbishop Charles Colet was aware of the movement of the Devotion throughout the United States, and he determined that it was time to appeal to the Pope for the Brief which would validate and perpetuate the Work of the Holy Face forever. However, as he set out to perform the task which he had set before himself, he became sick, and after a brief illness he passed away leaving the devotees of the Holy Face worried about what the next Bishop would do.

But they didn't have long to wait! The newly installed Archbishop of Tours, William Meignan, quickly issued a lengthy Ordinance establishing The Confraternity of the Holy Face in the Oratory on the Rue St. Etienne, and a few months later he had secured, from the Supreme Pontiff, an apostolic letter granting special indulgences to the members of the Confraternity. He then determined it was time to ask the Holy See for a Brief that would raise the Confraternity to the rank of an Archconfraternity to insure it in perpetuity.

With nearly sixty signatures, including bishops and a cardinal from America, on a petition to Pope Leo XIII, the Devotion to the Holy Face was destined to become a very integral part of Divine worship in the Church. Soon present at an audience with the Holy Father, the Prefect of the Sacred Congregation of Rites, asked if the title of Archconfraternity could be granted for all of France, to which Pope Leo XIII responded without hesitation: "Non tam pro Gallia, quam ubique!" "Not only for all of France, but for the whole world!" Rome had spoken, and the mission of Sr. Marie de St. Pierre and the desire of Leo Dupont had been realized.

On April 27, 1910, Pope Saint Pius X would approve the Feast of the Image of the Holy Face, with Rite of greater Double in the Third Feria, after the Sunday of Quinquagesima (Shrove Tuesday) for the diocese of Cambrai, France.

The Work of Reparation through Devotion to the Holy Face had the full approval of the Church.

So was erected in perpetuity, the Archconfraternity of Reparation in the Oratory of Leo Dupont, in 1885. There, to this day, priests still carry on the mission of Sister Mary of St. Peter, to whom Our Lord revealed over 100 years ago the real weapon that is destined to overthrow Communism. That weapon is the devotion to the Holy Face of Jesus, as a means of Reparation for the outrageous crimes of modern freethinkers, atheists, blasphemers, (Satanists), and the profaners of the Lord's Day. (These are the evils that more than any other cry to Heaven for vengeance, and that today bring us face to face with the threat of nuclear war, whose consequence would admittedly be the destruction of all civilization as we know it.)

The venerated Mr. Dupont, known in France and in Foreign countries under the designation of the Holy Man of Tours, was the restorer of the worship of the Holy Face in our midst.

His cherished memory, the examples, and the traditions he bequeathed to us, have been the means of inspiring the author of this manual, who is continuing in our sight, the fruitful and salutary work of his holy predecessor, with a generosity of soul corresponding to our desires and to the exceptional favors granted by Leo XIII happily reigning.

+ Guillaume,
Archbishop of Tours

(From the *Manual of the Archconfraternity of the Holy Face*, 1886)

Leo Dupont's canonization was presented to the Congregation for the Cause of Saints in 1939. The Holy See later declared him Venerable, and he now awaits beatification. His feast day is December 1st. and was declared Venerable by Pope Pius XII.

Prayer to Honor Venerable Leo Dupont

ETERNAL Father, I wish to honor Venerable Leo Dupont, and I give Thee thanks for all the graces Thou hast bestowed upon him. I ask Thee to please increase grace in my soul through the merits of this saint, and I commit the end of my life to him by this special prayer, so that by virtue of Thy goodness and promise, Venerable Leo Dupont might be my advocate and provide whatever is needed at that hour. Amen.

THE BRIEFS OF POPE LEO XIII

FIRST BRIEF OF THE HOLY FATHER

According special Indulgences to the Confraternity of the Holy Face

(Translation)

Leo XIII Pope.

For a perpetual remembrance.

Having learnt that, in a public Oratory of the town of Tours, dedicated to the Holy Face of our Lord Jesus Christ, there exists a pious association of the faithful, Legitimately Established under the title of the Holy Face:

In order that this association may receive great increase day by day; Putting all our confidence in the mercy of Almighty God, ad in the authority of his Blessed Apostles Peter and Paul, we grant:

I. To each and all the faithful of both sexes who shall enter into the said association, *a plenary indulgence* and the remission of all their sins on the first day of their entrance into the association, on condition that, being truly contrite and having confessed, they shall receive the most holy Sacrament of the Eucharist.

II. To such as shall have been already inscribed, or who shall be successively inscribed in the aforesaid association, a similar *plenary indulgence* at the article of death, provided that, being truly contrite, they confess and communicate, or if unable to do so, they at least, in a contrite spirit, devoutly invoke with their lips, or if that be not possible, with their heart, the Holy Name of Jesus.

III. To all and each of the brethren and sisters who are already, or who shall henceforward become members of the said association, a *plenary indulgence* on the feast of St. Peter, the prince of the apostles and the principal patron of the Confraternity, whether it be on the day itself of his feast, or at their pleasure on one of the seven days immediately following, provided that, being truly penitent, and having confessed and communicated, they devoutly visit the above mentioned Oratory, and that they there piously offer to God prayers for the concord of Christian princes, the extirpation of heresies, the conversion of sinners in the exaltation of holy mother Church.

IV. To the same persons, a similar *plenary indulgence* every year, on a day which must be fixed by the Ordinary, provided that they visit the above-named Oratory fulfilling the conditions already mentioned, from the first vespers of that day to the setting of the sun (1);

In addition, we grant to the same members of the faithful, according to the usual form of the Church, an *indulgence of 60 days* for the remission of penances which have been enjoined upon them, or which they have merited on any occasion whatever:

I.   Each time that, having at least a contrite heart, they shall devoutly assist at some pious exercise in the above-named Oratory;

II. Each time that they shall piously kiss the sorrowful Face of Christ, the distinctive sign of their Confraternity, whether it be sculptured, or whether it be engraved or impressed upon a cross or a picture, adding this invocation: *Lord, show us Thy Face, and we shall be saved.*

III. Lastly, each time that they shall perform some other pious, or charitable act, in conformity with the object of their Confraternity.

We grant in the Lord, that all and every one of these Indulgences, remissions of sins and dispensations of penance, may be applied, by way of suffrage, to the souls of the faithful who have departed out of this world united to God through charity.

These presents have a value in perpetuity for the future.

Given at Rome, near St. Peter, under the ring of the fisherman, the 9th of December 1884, being the 7th year of our Pontificate.

Place of the seal.

For Monseigneur Cardinal

Chisi,

O. Princhieri, *substitute.*

Examined and certified:

Tours, 16th December 1884.

Durand, vic. Gen.

Source: Manual of the Archconfraternity of the Holy Face, 1887

SECOND BRIEF OF THE HOLY FATHER

(Translation)

Leo XIII Pope.

For a perpetual remembrance.

We have been informed that, by our apostolical letters, dated 9th of December 1884, plenary and partial Indulgences were accorded to the pious Confraternity of the Holy Face, canonically established in the town of Tours. This said Confraternity has now addressed a petition to us, requesting that, for the greater spiritual good of the faithful and the salvation of souls, we would deign to enrich it still more by fresh treasures of celestial gifts. Therefore, acceding to this pious request and being charged to open with tender charity the heavenly treasures of the Church, in order to promote the faith of our people and the salvation of souls;

I. We mercifully grant in the Lord, every year, on the day of the feast of the Transfiguration of our Lord Jesus Christ, or on any one of the days of the octave which may be fixed upon, *a plenary indulgence* and the remission of all their sins to the faithful who are now, or who may henceforth become members of the above named Confraternity, provided that being sincerely penitent, and having confessed and communicated, they shall devoutly visit the public Oratory dedicated to the Holy Face in the town of Tours, and that they there pray for the concord of Christian princes, the extirpation of heresies, the conversion of sinners and the exaltation of holy mother Church;

II. Moreover to the same faithful, who, on any day whatever of the year which they shall choose, shall make a pilgrimage to the Oratory, whether in groups or singly, and shall there devoutly visit the picture of the Holy Face, and shall receive holy Communion and shall there in the manner stated above, we also grant, in the Lord, once a year, a *plenary indulgence*, in the remission of all their sins;

III. In addition, to the same associates, who, being at least of contrite heart, shall assist at monthly meeting of the Confraternity, held either in the above-mentioned Oratory, or in any church whatever, we remit in accordance with the usual form, *7 years and 7 quarantines* of the penances which may have been enjoined upon them, or which are otherwise obligatory upon them, in any manner soever.

IV. We also consent that all and each one of these Indulgences, remissions of sins and dispensations from penances, may be applied, by way of suffrage, to the souls of the faithful who have departed from this world, united to God, by charity.

V. Lastly, by the tenour of these presents, we give to the above mentioned associates the faculty, if the weak state of their health prevents them from visiting their Oratory, in order to gain the *plenary or partial indulgences,* the power, freely and lawfully, with the permission and according t the judgment of their confessor, to change this act of piety for some other good work.

These presents are valid for 7 years only.

Given at Rome, near St. Peter, under the seal of the fisherman, the 30th March, 1885, being the 8th year of our Pontificate.

Place of the Seal.

Cardinal Ledochowski

Examined and permitted to be executed:

Tours, 22nd, April 1885.

J. Buisson, vic. gen.

Source: Manual of the Archconfraternity of the Holy Face, 1887.

THIRD BRIEF OF THE HOLY FATHER

Brief of his Holiness Pope Leo XIII

ESTABLISHING THE ARCHCONFRATERNITY OF THE HOLY FACE

Leo XIII Pope.

For a Perpetual Remembrance.

According to the usages of Roman Pontiffs, our predecessors, we are accustomed to decorate and enrich with special honors and privileges the pious associations instituted for the practice of works of piety and charity. Our beloved sons, the directors and associates of the pious Confraternity known as that of the Holy Face, canonically established in the sanctuary of the same name, in the town of Tours, and enriched by us and the Holy See with numerous privileges, have expressed to us the desire, that making use of the plenitude of our apostolic power, we should honor this association with the title of Archconfraternity and with the preeminence which is its due.

Desirous of giving to each and all of those in whose favor these letters are delivered a special mark of our benevolence, and only as regards the present case, considering them has absolved, and to be absolved from all sentences of excommunication and interdict, and from all the censures and ecclesiastical penalties which they may have incurred and which may have been inflicted on them in any manner or for any cause whatsoever, we, by our apostolical authority, in virtue of these presents, establish and constitute as a perpetual Archconfraternity, with the accustomed privileges, the so-called Confraternity of the Holy Face, established in the town of Tours.

And by the same our authority, in virtue of these letters, we concede in grant in perpetuity, to the directors and colleagues present and future of the Archconfraternity, the power, validly and lawfully, to aggregate to itself, throughout the whole world, excepting in our glorious city, all the other Confraternities existing in the same name and having the same object, observing always the form prescribed by the Constitution of Pope Clement VIII, our predecessor of happy memory, and the other apostolical ordinances drawn up on the subject, as well as to communicate to all and each the Indulgences, remissions of sins and dispensations of penance, which have been granted by the Holy Apostolical See to the association so erected by us into the Archconfraternity, and which are susceptible of being communicated to others.

We decree that our present letters shall be, for the present and the future, fixed, valid and efficacious; that they shall obtain and possess their full and entire effects, that they shall fully favor all and for all, whom they concern and shall concern hereafter in accordance with what has been previously enumerated, and shall be judged and defined by ordinary judges and delegates, whoever they may be, even the auditors of the suits of the apostolic Palace, the Nuncios of the Holy See, the Cardinals of the Holy Roman Church, even legates *a latere* and all other personages, whatever their dignity and their power may be; entire power and authority to judge and interpret otherwise being withdrawn from them in general and in particular, so that if anyone, whatever be the authority with which he is invested, attacks any of these causes knowingly or through ignorance, his act shall be null and void.

And this notwithstanding the Constitutions and Apostolic ordinances, and, in as far as is necessary, the statutes, customs and uses contrary to the above-named Confraternity and all others soever, even when they have been confirmed by apostolic oath or any other decision whatever.

Given at Rome, near St. Peter, under the ring of the fisherman, the 1st day of October 1885, being the 8th year of our Pontificate.

Place of the seal.

Cardinal Ledochowski.

Examined,

We command its execution and use

Guillaume-Ren,

Archbishop of Tours.

Place of the Seal

Source: Manual of the Archconfraternity of the Holy Face, 1887.

INDULGENCES GRANTED BY LEO XIII
(Applicable to the souls in Purgatory)

PLENARY INDULGENCES

1. On the day of admission;

2. At the hour of death;

3. For every yearly pilgrimage made to the Oratory of the Holy Face

4. On the feast of St. Peter, or on a day during the Octave;

5. On the feast of the Transfiguration, only day during the Octave;

6. On Passion Sunday, or any other day fixed by the Ordinary.

In order to gain these last 3 Indulgences, it is necessary to visit the seat of their Confraternity.

PARTIAL INDULGENCES – *7 years and 7 quarantines* for each assistance at the monthly reunions.

60 days: 1. For each pious exercise performed at the seat of the Confraternity; 2. For any other work of piety offered in union with the object of the Association; 3. Each time a member devoutly kisses the effigy of the Holy Face repeating the invocation: *Lord, show us Thy Face, and we shall be saved.*

100 days for every prayer said before in effigy of the Holy Face. *(Pius IX, December 11, 1876.)*

40 days each time a member assists at any of the daily morning or evening exercises in the chapel of the Holy Face at Tours. *(The Archbishop of Tours, November 15th 1876.*

The above Indulgences which require that a visit should be made to the church, maybe gained by sick persons by virtue of some other act prescribed by the confessor. (Brief of the 30th March 1885.)

N.B. – The associates will endeavor to be faithful to their pious engagements, although these engagements, as they all know, do not impose an obligation of conscience, that is to say, do not oblige under penalty of sin.

ADVICE TO THE ASSOCIATES

I. To wear on their persons a picture of the Holy Face, to kiss it devoutly the 1st thing in the morning on awaking and at night before going to sleep, to consecrate their actions during the day to the divine Face, to resolve to perform them in its presence and before its eyes.

II. At the commencement of their prayers, or of any exercise of piety, has an easy means of placing themselves in the presence of God, and of combating distractions, to thing of the Holy Face whose eyes are open and fixed upon us, to adore it with faith, to look at it with love.

III. In the presence of the Blessed Sacrament, to recall to our remembrance the fact that the Face of the Savior is present there in the Sacred Host: that it sees us, listens to us, blesses us, speaks to us interiorly.

IV. To endeavor in their conduct to imitate the virtues of patience, of gentleness, of serenity, of modesty, which shine in the Holy Face. Listen to the Divine Master who said learn of me, and seeing me, *that I am meek* in face and *humble of heart*: knowing that, in fact the gentleness and humility of the heart of Jesus are, as in a very clear mirror, admirably reflected on the Face of the Man God.

V. In trials, sicknesses, accidents, temptations, to prostrate themselves before the picture of the Holy Face whether in their private Oratory, or above all, in the church of the Confraternity where it is specially exposed.

VI. To have in their houses a picture of the Holy Face which they shall honor as the protector of the family and the Guardian of the domestic hearth; to recite before it the prayers which are habitually said in common by the household.

VII. When they shall hear any blasphemies pronounced or shall see and act of impious sacrilege which they cannot prevent, to recollect themselves and to pronounce with their hearts, if they cannot with their lips, the words: Behold, O God, our Protector, and look upon the Face of Thy Christ, or: May the Name of the Lord be blessed! *Sit Nomen Domini benedictum!*

VIII. To propagate the worship of the Holy Face in their locality, amongst their friends and acquaintances, and to make use of it in order to combat, in every possible manner, the terrible effects of indifference and irreligion.

Source: Manual of the Archconfraternity of the Holy Face, 1887.

PRAYERS

OF THE

HOLY FACE DEVOTION

Prayers of Reparation

Morning Offering

Eternal Father, through the Sorrowful and Immaculate Heart of Mary, I offer to you the Most Precious Blood of Jesus and the Holy Face of Jesus on all the altars throughout the world, and offering with them my every thought, word, and action of this day. Oh, my Jesus, I desire to gain every indulgence and merit that I can, offering them together with myself to Mary Immaculate, who is the dispenser of the Merits of Thy Most Precious Blood. Precious Blood of Jesus, save us; Our Lady of Mt. Carmel, pray for us; Sacred Heart of Jesus, have mercy on us.

Salutation
To the Holy Relic of the Vatican Basilica
Antiphon

My heart speaks to Thee; my eyes seek Thee; yes, Lord, I will always seek Thy Face. Do not hide Thy Face from me; do not turn away from Thy servant.

V. O Lord, Thou hast shown to me the light of Thy Face.
R. Thou hast given joy to my heart.

Grant in Thy Mercy, O Lord, that my soul, created by Thy wisdom and governed by Thy providence, may be filled with the light of Thy Holy Face, through our Lord Jesus Christ. Amen.

The Golden Arrow

May the most holy, most sacred,
most adorable, most incomprehensible
and unutterable Name of God
be always praised, blessed, loved,
adored, and glorified in Heaven,
on earth, and under the earth,
by all the creatures of God,
and by the Sacred Heart of Our Lord,
Jesus Christ, in the most
Holy Sacrament of the Altar. Amen.

Nihil obstat
C. L. Mulholland
Feb. 29, 1956

Imprimatur:
+ T.K. Gorman, D.D.
Bishop of Dallas – Fort Worth

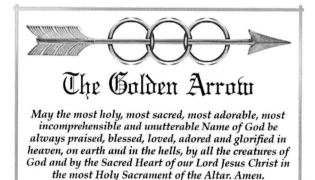

The Golden Arrow

May the most holy, most sacred, most adorable, most incomprehensible and unutterable Name of God be always praised, blessed, loved, adored and glorified in heaven, on earth and in the hells, by all the creatures of God and by the Sacred Heart of our Lord Jesus Christ in the most Holy Sacrament of the Altar. Amen.

Litany of the Holy Face
In Reparation for Blasphemies

Lord, *have mercy on us.*
Jesus Christ, *have mercy on us.*
Lord, *have mercy on us.*
Jesus Christ, *hear us.*
Jesus Christ, *graciously hear us.*
Holy Virgin Mary, *pray for us.*

O Adorable Face, adored with profound respect by Mary and Joseph when they saw Thee for the first time; *have mercy on us. Gloria (Glory Be)*

O Adorable Face, which in the stable of Bethlehem didst ravish with joy the Angels, the shepherds, and the wise men; *have mercy on us. Gloria…*

O Adorable Face, which in the Temple didst transpierce with a dart of love the saintly Simeon and the prophetess Anna; *have mercy on us. Gloria…*

O **Adorable Face,** which wast bathed in tears in Thy holy infancy; *have mercy on us. Gloria...*

O **Adorable Face,** which appearing in the Temple, didst fill with admiration the Doctors of the Law; *have mercy on us. Gloria...*

O **Adorable Face,** whose charms were so ravishing, and whose grace was so attractive; *have mercy on us. Gloria...*

O **Adorable Face,** whose nobility characterized every feature; *have mercy on us. Gloria...*

O **Adorable Face,** contemplated by the Angels; *have mercy on us. Gloria...*

O **Adorable Face,** sweet delight of the Saints; *have mercy on us. Gloria...*

O **Adorable Face,** masterpiece of the Holy Ghost, in which the Eternal Father is well pleased; *have mercy on us. Gloria...*

O **Adorable Face,** delight of Mary and Joseph; *have mercy on us. Gloria...*

O **Adorable Face,** ineffable mirror of the divine perfections; *have mercy on us. Gloria...*

O **Adorable Face,** which appeasest the anger of God; *have mercy on us. Gloria...*

O **Adorable Face,** which makest the devils tremble; *have mercy on us. Gloria...*

O **Adorable Face,** treasure of grace and blessings; *have mercy on us. Gloria...*

O Adorable Face, exposed in the desert to the inclemencies of the weather; *have mercy on us. Gloria...*

O Adorable Face, which wast bathed with sweat in Thy journeys and scorched with the heat and sun; *have mercy on us. Gloria...*

O Adorable Face, whose expression was all divine; *have mercy on us. Gloria...*

O Adorable Face, whose modesty and meekness attracted both just and sinners; *have mercy on us. Gloria...*

O Adorable Face, troubled and weeping at the tomb of Lazarus; *have mercy on us. Gloria...*

O Adorable Face, brilliant as the sun and radiant with glory on Mount Thabor; *have mercy on us. Gloria...*

O Adorable Face, sorrowful at the sight of Jerusalem and shedding tears over that ungrateful city; *have mercy on us. Gloria...*

O Adorable Face, bowed to the earth in the Garden of Olives and covered with confusion for our sins; *have mercy on us. Gloria...*

O Adorable Face, bathed in a bloody sweat; *have mercy on us. Gloria...*

O Adorable Face, kissed by the traitor Judas, *have mercy on us. Gloria...*

O Adorable Face, whose sanctity and majesty struck the soldiers with fear and cast them to the ground; *have mercy on us. Gloria...*

O Adorable Face, struck by an infamous servant, blindfolded, and profaned by the sacrilegious hands of thine enemies; *have mercy on us. Gloria...*

O **Adorable Face**, defiled with spittle and bruised by so many buffets and blows; *have mercy on us. Gloria…*

O **Adorable Face**, whose divine look wounded the heart of Peter with repentant sorrow and love; *have mercy on us. Gloria…*

O **Adorable Face**, humbled for us at the tribunals of Jerusalem; *have mercy on us. Gloria…*

O **Adorable Face**, which didst preserve Thy serenity when Pilate pronounced the fatal sentence; *have mercy on us. Gloria…*

O **Adorable Face**, covered with sweat and blood, and falling into the mire under the weight of the cross; *have mercy on us. Gloria…*

O **Adorable Face**, wiped with a veil by a pious woman on the road to Calvary; *have mercy on us. Gloria…*

O **Adorable Face**, raised on the instrument of the most shameful punishment; *have mercy on us. Gloria…*

O **Adorable Face**, whose incomparable beauty was obscured under the fearful cloud of the sins of the world; *have mercy on us. Gloria…*

O **Adorable Face**, covered with the sad shades of death; *have mercy on us. Gloria…*

O **Adorable Face**, washed and anointed by Mary and the holy women, and covered with a shroud; *have mercy on us. Gloria…*

O **Adorable Face**, enclosed in the sepulcher; *have mercy on us. Gloria…*

O **Adorable Face**, all resplendent with glory and beauty on the day of the resurrection; *have mercy on us. Gloria…*

O Adorable Face, all dazzling with light at the moment of Thy ascension; *have mercy on us. Gloria…*

O Adorable Face, hidden in the Eucharist; *have mercy on us. Gloria…*

O Adorable Face, which wilt appear at the end of time in the clouds, with great power and majesty; *have mercy on us. Gloria…*

O Adorable Face, which wilt cause sinners to tremble; *have mercy on us. Gloria…*

O Adorable Face, which wilt fill the just with joy for all eternity; *have mercy on us. Gloria…*

Lamb of God, who takest away the sins of the world, *spare us, O Lord.*

Lamb of God, who takest away the sins of the world, *graciously hear us, O Lord.*

Lamb of God, who takest away the sins of the world, *have mercy on us, O Lord.*

Let us pray

I salute, adore, and love Thee, O Jesus, my Savior, covered anew with outrages by blasphemers, and I offer Thee, through the heart of Thy Blessed Mother, the worship of all the angels and saints, as an incense and a perfume of sweet odor, most humbly beseeching Thee, by the virtue of Thy Holy Face, to repair and renew in me and in all men, Thine image disfigured by sin. Amen.

Say an Our Father, a Hail Mary, and a Glory Be.

A Most Efficacious Novena

Say the Golden Arrow, the Litany of the Holy Face and the Chaplet of the Holy Face for nine days.

Eternal God, we implore You,
by the
Adorable Face of Your Son,
the
conversion of blasphemers.
Amen.

Prayer to Reproduce the
Image of God in Our Souls

When practicing the Holy Face Devotion offer,
in your prayers to the Eternal Father, the
Most Holy Face of Jesus as a *Priceless Coin of Infinite Value:*

'Just as in an earthly kingdom, money,
which is stamped with the picture of the
sovereign or ruling executive of the country
procures whatever one desires to purchase,
so likewise, in the Kingdom of Heaven, you
shall obtain all that you desire by offering the
coin of My Precious Humanity which is My
Adorable Face.'

- Our Lord to Sr. Mary of St. Peter-

Novena
Praise Petition and Thanksgiving
to the
Most Holy Face

O Lord Jesus Christ, in presenting
ourselves before Thy Adorable Face
to ask of Thee the graces of which we
stand most in need, we beseech
Thee above all, to give us that interior
disposition of never refusing at any
time to do what Thou requirest of us
by Thy Holy Commandments and
Thy Divine Inspirations.

O Good Jesus, Who has said: "Ask and
you shall receive, seek and you shall find,
knock and it shall be opened to you,
grant us, by the pure effect of Thy
charity and for Thy eternal glory, the
graces we need and which we look for
from Thine infinite mercy,
particularly ___, (ask Our Lord through
the merits of
His Most Holy Face.) Amen.

Be Merciful to us, O God, and reject
not our prayers when, amid our afflictions,
we call upon Thy Holy Name
and seek with Love and confidence
Thine Adorable Face. Amen.

We thank Thee, O Lord, for all Thy
benefits, and we entreat Thee to
engrave in our hearts feelings
of love and gratitude, putting upon
our lips songs of thanksgiving
to Thine eternal praise. Amen.

The Divine Praises
In
Reparation for Blasphemies

Blessed be God.
Blessed be His Holy Name.
Blessed be Jesus Christ, true God and true Man.
Blessed be the Name of Jesus.
Blessed be His Most Sacred Heart.
Blessed be His Most Precious Blood.
Blessed be Jesus in the Most Holy Sacrament of the Altar.
Blessed be the Holy Ghost the Paraclete.
Blessed be the great Mother of God, Mary most holy.
Blessed be her Holy and Immaculate Conception.
Blessed be her glorious Assumption.
Blessed be St. Joseph, her most chaste spouse.
Blessed be God in His Angels and in His saints.

Praises of the Holy Face

Blessed be Jesus!
Blessed be the Holy Face in the majesty and beauty of Its heavenly features!
Blessed be the Holy Face through the words which issued from Its divine mouth!
Blessed be the Holy Face through all the glances which escaped from Its adorable eyes!
Blessed be the Holy Face in the Transfiguration of Tabor!
Blessed be the Holy Face in the fatigues of Its apostolate!
Blessed be the Holy Face in the bloody sweat of the agony!
Blessed be the Holy Face in the humiliations of the Passion!
Blessed be the Holy Face in the sufferings of death!
Blessed be the Holy Face in the splendor of the Resurrection!
Blessed be the Holy Face in the glory of light eternal!

Prayers of Sister Marie de St. Pierre

I salute You, I adore You, and I love You, O Jesus, my Savior, outraged anew by blasphemers, and I offer You, through the heart of Your Blessed Mother, the worship of all the angels and saints, as an incense and a perfume of sweet odor, most humbly beseeching You, by the virtue of Your Sacred Face, to repair and renew in me and in all men Your image disfigured by sin. Amen. **(Our Father, Hail Mary, Glory Be)**

O Adorable Face of my JESUS, so mercifully bowed down upon the tree of the cross on the day of Your Passion for the salvation of men, now again, incline in Your pity towards us poor sinners. Cast upon us a look of compassion and receive us to the kiss of peace. Amen.

Sacred Heart of Jesus, have mercy on us. Amen.
May the Name of the Lord be blessed! Amen.

Eternal Father, we offer You the adorable Face of Your well-beloved Son for the honor and glory of Your Holy Name and for the salvation of all men. Amen.

Sister Marie de St. Pierre's Prayer
to the
Queen of Carmel for the Houses of Her Order

"Oh, Holy Mary, sprinkle the flowers of Carmel with thy fruitful grace, that they may thus become so strongly rooted in this land of benediction as never to be eradicated by the demon."

The 'O Gloriosa Virginum' repeat seventy-two times in honor of her Divine Maternity.

Come, Jesus, come! *Sit Nomen Domini benedictum.*

Mother most pure, pray for us. Oh Mary, Mother of God, source of all our joy for time and eternity, be thou our strength. Lead us to the arms of thy Divine Child and teach us His winning ways. When earth and sense shall fail show us thy gentle face, and in thy pure embrace let us meet the merciful gaze of our Saviour Jesus. Amen.

Prayers of Venerable Leo Dupont

Adorable Face of my Jesus, my only Love, my Light, and my Life, grant that I may see, know, and love You alone, and that I may live by You and for You. Amen.

O Lord Jesus Christ, in presenting ourselves before Your Adorable Face, to ask of You the graces of which we stand most in need, we beseech You, above all, to give us that interior disposition of never refusing at any time to do what You require of us by Your commandments and divine inspirations. Amen.

O Good Jesus, who has said: "Ask and you shall receive, seek, and you shall find, knock and it shall be opened to you," give us, O Lord, that faith which obtains all, or supply in us what may be deficient; grant us, by the pure effect of Your charity, and for Your eternal glory, the graces which we need and which we look for from Your infinite mercy. Amen.

Be merciful to us, O my God, and reject not our prayers, when amid our afflictions we call on Your Holy Name and seek with love and confidence Your Adorable Face. Amen.

We bless You, O Lord, for all Your benefits, and beseech You to imprint in our hearts sentiments of love and gratitude, putting into our mouths songs of thanksgiving to Your eternal praise. Amen.

May I expire, burning with an ardent thirst to see the adorable Face of our Lord Jesus Christ! (This prayer of Saint Edmund was repeated often by Venerable Leo Dupont during the latter portion of his life.)

Prayers Used by Venerable Leo Dupont
When Anointing the Sick with Holy Oil

May the Lord Himself deign, together with us, to anoint this sick person and to restore him to health. In the name of the Father, and of the Son, and of the Holy Ghost. Amen.

May the Holy Names of Jesus, of Mary, and of St. Joseph be known, blest, and glorified throughout the whole earth. Amen.

Blessed Oil obtained from the
Shrine of the
Holy Face in Tours, France

Aspirations

Eternal Father, I offer You the Body and Blood of our Lord Jesus Christ, in expiation for our sins and for the needs of Holy Church.

Amiable Heart of Jesus, our Mediator, appease Your Father, and save sinners.

*Powerful Heart of Mary, refuge of sinners,
stay the arrows of divine justice.*

Say Often Throughout the Day

Eternal Father, we offer You the Holy Face of Jesus covered with blood, sweat, dust and spittle, in reparation for the crimes of communists, blasphemers, and for the profaners of the Holy Name and of the Holy Day of Sunday. Amen.

FORTY DAYS' PRAYER
For the Needs of the Church and State
Commenced by Venerable Leo Dupont 1843

May God arise, and His enemies be dispersed! (Say three Pater Nosters, three Ave Marias, and three Gloria Patris)

St. Michael and all the holy Angels, pray and combat for us.

St. Peter and all the holy Apostles, intercede for us.

St. Ignatius, St. Teresa, and all the inhabitants of the Heavenly Jerusalem, pray for us.

Act of Reparation

I adore You, and I praise You, O my Divine Jesus, Son of the living God, for all the outrages You have endured for me, who am the most miserable of Your creatures, in all the sacred members of Your body, but especially in the most noble part Yourself, that is to say, in Your Face. I salute You, amiable Face, wounded with blows and scourges, soiled with spittle and disfigured by the evil treatment which impious sinners caused you to suffer.

I salute you, oh lovely eyes, all bathed in the tears you have shed for our salvation. I salute you, oh sacred ears, tormented by an infinity of blasphemies, injuries and shameful mockings. I salute you, oh holy mouth, filled with grace and sweetness towards sinners and made to drink vinegar and gall by the monstrous ingratitude of those whom You have chosen to be Your people. In reparation for all these ignominies, I offer You all the homage which has been rendered You in the holy places where You have willed to be honored by the special devotion to which I unite myself with my whole heart. Amen.

An Act of Honorable Amends

To the Most Holy Face of Our Lord Jesus Christ. In reparation for the sin of blasphemy, of the profanation of Sundays and of other impious crimes against God and the Church.

Most holy and most Adorable Face of our Savior, humbly prostrate in Your presence, we present ourselves before You, in order, by a solemn act of faith and of piety, to render You the homage of veneration, praise, and love which is Your due. We also desire to offer to You honorable amends and a public reparation for the sins, blasphemies and sacrileges of which the present generation has rendered itself culpable towards the Divine Majesty, and which, in regard to You, Oh well-beloved Face, renew the ignominies and the sufferings of Your Passion.

It is with terror and profound affliction that we are witnesses of these monstrous crimes, which cannot fail to draw down upon society and upon our families, the malediction and the chastisements of Divine Justice. We see, in fact, all around us the law of the Lord and the authority of His Church despised and trodden under foot; His thrice Holy Name denied or blasphemed; the Sunday, which He has reserved for His worship, publicly profaned; His altars and His offices forsaken for criminal of frivolous pleasures. The impious attack all that is sacred and religious. But it is, above all, the Divinity of Christ, the Son of the living God; it is the Incarnate Word; it is the August Face and the Crucifix which they attack with the greatest fury; the spit and the blows of His persecutors are renewed by the insults and the outrages which their hatred dares, in every possible manner, to inflict upon You, Oh Face, full of sweetness and of love.

Pardon, a thousand times pardon, for all these crimes! May we make amends for them by our humble supplications and the fervor of our homage. But, guilty and sinners as we are, what can we offer the Eternal Father in order to appease His just anger, if it be not Yourself, Oh Sorrowful Face, who has deigned to make Yourself our advocate and our victim? Supply what may be wanting in us by Your satisfactions and Your merits.

Heavenly Father, we entreat You, "look on the Face of Your Christ." Behold the wounds which disfigure It, the tears which escape from Its sunken eyes; the sweat with which It is bathed; the blood which flows in streams down Its profaned and wounded cheeks. Behold also Its invincible patience. Its unalterable gentleness, Its infinite tenderness and Its merciful goodness towards sinners. This Holy Face is turned towards You, and before exhaling Its last sigh, lovingly inclined upon the Cross, It implores You in favor of those who curse and outrage It.

Oh Father, listen to that suppliant cry, permit Yourself to be touched; have pity on us and pardon us. Grant, moreover, that in the presence of this Divine Face, equally formidable and powerful, the enemies of Your Name may take flight and disappear; that they may be converted and live!

May the most adorable Name of God be adored forever and ever!

May Sundays and all Holy days of the Lord be sanctified by all men!

May the Holy Face of Jesus be loved by every heart!

May the Holy Church, our Mother, be exalted throughout the whole earth!

May our holy Father, the Pope, Vicar of Jesus Christ, be venerated by all people!

St. Peter, Prince of the Apostles, and Patron of the Archconfraternity, pray for us!

Lord, show us Your Face, and we shall be saved Amen! Amen!

Prayer of Pope Pius IX

Oh, my Jesus! Cast upon us a look of mercy; turn Your Face towards each of us as You did to Veronica; not that we may see It with our bodily eyes, for this we do not deserve; but turn It towards our hearts, so that, remembering You, we may ever draw from this fountain of strength the vigor necessary to sustain the combats of life. Amen.

Our lady of the Holy Name of God, may thou be blessed in all times and all places.

Cry of Love

Pardon, pardon, O my God, for the innumerable souls which are being lost every day around us. The devil rushes forth from the abyss, hurrying to make horrible conquests; he excites the infernal band; he exclaims – Souls! Souls! Let us hasten to ruin souls! – and souls fall like autumn leaves into the eternal abyss.

We also, oh, my God, will cry – Souls! Souls! We must have souls, wherewith to acquit the debt of gratitude we have contracted towards You; we ask them of You by the wounds of Jesus, our Savior. These adorable wounds cry out to You even as so many powerful mouths. The King crowned with thorns demands subjects torn from the devil; we ask them of You, together with Him and by Him, for Your greater glory, and by the intercession of the most Holy Virgin Mary, conceived without sin.

PRAYER TO THE BLESSED VIRGIN MARY

We beseech You, Oh Lord, in Your infinite goodness to free us from the bonds of our sins, and through the intercession of the ever-blessed Virgin Mary, Mother of God, together with Your holy apostles Peter and Paul, and all the saints to keep us, Your children, and our household in all holiness. Cleanse our relatives, friends, and companions from all their offences and shower them with Your virtues. Give us Your peace and salvation; deliver us from our enemies, visible and invisible, and restrain our sinful inclinations. Grant us favorable weather and bestow Your love upon our friends and enemies.

Guard Your Holy City and its chief Ruler, our Holy Father N. N. Watch over all the ministers of Your Church and keep rulers and all Christian people from every adversity.

May Your blessing be always upon us and may the souls of the faithful departed rest in peace. Through our Lord Jesus Christ. Amen.

Prayer of St. Therese of the Child Jesus
and of the Holy Face
For Sinners

Eternal Father, since You have given me for my inheritance the adorable Face of Your Divine Son, I offer that Face to You, and I beg You, in exchange for this coin of infinite value, to forget the ingratitude of souls dedicated to You, and to pardon all poor sinners.

All prayers in this book have been copied from approved sources.

CONSECRATION TO THE HOLY FACE
For the use of Members of the Confraternity
of the Holy Face.

I .... In order to give still greater increase to
the glory of Jesus dying for our salvation upon the cross; in order to
correspond to the merciful love with which His Holy Face is
animated towards poor sinners, and in order to repair the outrages
which the frightful crimes of the present day inflict upon His august
Face, the most pure mirror of the Divine Majesty-associate myself,
fully and freely, to the faithful received into this pious confraternity;
I desire to participate in the indulgences with which it is enriched
and in the good works practiced therein, as well as for the expiation
of my sins and for the solace of souls suffering in Purgatory. Amiable
Redeemer, most sweet Jesus, hide in the secret of Your Face all the
members of this association; may they there find shelter from the
seductions of the world, and the snares of Satan; grant that ,
faithfully keeping all the precepts of Your Law and fulfilling the
special duties of their state, they may be more and more inflamed
with zeal for reparation, and with the flames of Your Divine Love.

Holy Face Devotion
St. Damien of Molokai Parish
Edmond, Oklahoma U.S.A.

SACRAMENTALS
OF THE
HOLY FACE DEVOTION

The Picture of the Holy Face
Adopted by the Confraternity

In preference to all other representations of the Holy Face of our Lord, the Confraternity chose the facsimile of the Veil of Veronica.

Reproduction of St. Veronica's Veil

The manual of the Archconfraternity of the Holy Face states:

> For long periods of time reproductions of the effigy of the Holy Face were forbidden. Since the "miracle of the Vatican" in 1849, however, the Sovereign Pontiffs have authorized printed copies of the Sacred Picture to be made on linen or silk. These are then impressed with a Cardinal's seal and furnished with a guarantee. The word "Gratis,"

printed on the picture, refers to the spiritual benefit, only of the effigy which has been touched to the Wood of the True Cross, the Sacred Lance and the Original effigy or miraculous picture of the Holy Face, venerated and kept for centuries with the major relics of the Basilica in the Vatican, Rome. Expositions or "ostensions" of It are made in the Vatican at least 13 times a year, and the blessing given is the same as that of the Blessed Sacrament. (This has been discontinued at present.)

Innumerable miracles have been worked with the original and its copies throughout the world. The faithful reproductions are permitted to be exposed in different parts of the world in order to reanimate faith and piety in the hearts of the people.

Holy Face picture given to the author
for promotion of the Holy Face Devotion
in Oklahoma by the
Discalced Carmelite Nuns
of the
Infant Jesus of Prague and St. Joseph Monastery
Dallas, Texas
Deo Gratias!

The Little Chaplet
of the
Holy Face

The little Chaplet of the Holy Face, composed by Sr. Marie de St. Pierre, has for its object the honoring of the five senses of our Lord Jesus Christ, and of entreating God for the Triumph of His Church.

This chaplet consists of a cross, thirty-nine beads, (six large and thirty-three small), and of a medal of the Holy Face. It is well to recite it every day, in order to obtain from God, by means of the Face of His Well-beloved Son, the triumph of our Mother the Catholic Church, and the downfall of her enemies.

The cross recalls to us the mystery of our Redemption. The thirty-three small beads represent the thirty-three years of the mortal life of our Lord. The first thirty, divided into five groups of six small beads, recall the thirty years of His private life, and each group is prayed with the intention of honoring the five senses of the touch, taste, sight, smell, and hearing of Jesus. These have their seat principally in His Holy Face, and the Chaplet is prayed rendering homage to all the suffering which our Lord endured in His Face, through each one of these senses. The last three small beads are prayed recalling the public life of the Savior and have for their object the honoring of all the wounds of His Face. Each large bead, which precedes all the groups of beads, has as its object, as well, of paying homage to all the wounds that Jesus suffered. The Gloria Patri is said on the 6 large beads.

The *Glory Be to the Father* (Gloria Patri) is recited seven times in honor of the seven last words of Jesus upon the Cross and the Seven Sorrows (Dolors) of the Immaculate Virgin.

How to say the Chaplet of the Holy Face

Sign yourself with the Cross and say:

Vs. O God, come to my assistance!
Rs. O Lord, make haste to help me! Glory be to the Father . . .

On the 6 large(single) beads say:

My Jesus Mercy! Glory be to the Father, and to the Son, and to the Holy Spirit, as it was in the beginning, is now and ever shall be, world without end. Amen.

On the 33 small beads say:

Vs. Arise, O Lord, and let Thy enemies be scattered
Rs. And let them that hate Thee, flee from before Thy Face.

On the medal (and thus concluding the Chaplet) say:

Vs. O God, our Protector, look on us.
Rs. And look on the Face of Thy Christ

Cross of the Holy Face

Sister Marie de St. Pierre: "Our Lord told me that
He desired each member of the Association to wear a special
cross, and that on one side of this cross should be engraved with
the words, "Blessed be the Name of God," and on the reverse
side should be the words, "Begone, Satan".

To all those wearing this holy cross our Lord promised a
special resourcefulness to conquer the demon of blasphemy
adding that every time one hears a curse, he should repeat the
two short inscriptions written on each side of the cross, and he
will thus overcome the evil one and render glory to God."

On the Feast of the Purification, February 2nd, 1844, our Lord
offers a promise of pardon in view of the efforts made to spread
the Reparation. He further designates Saint Michael, Saint Martin,
and St. Louis as the special patrons of the Work, and asks that the
members wear a cross, and band themselves together as "Defenders of
God's Holy Name."

The Archconfraternity Cross
of the Holy Face
Taken from the Manual of the
Archconfraternity of the Holy Face, 1887

The Archconfraternity, having its center in the archiepiscopal city of Tours where it had its origin, adopts as a principal sign of decoration for its members a cross with two arms arranged in the manner shown in the engraving given above; on the center of one of its sides is inscribed the monogram of Christ surrounded with the words: Pius IX. 1847, and upon the arms of the cross, engraved with the picture of **Christ's Face on Veronica's Veil**, are the words **"Sit Nomen Domini Benedictum"** and on the back: **"Vade retro, Satana"**.

Associates are advised habitually to wear this cross as a safeguard; during pilgrimages and at public ceremonies, it is well to have it placed where it can be seen on the breast. The Archconfraternity is an army; the cross, such as it has been described, is its standard; let us wear it with confidence; it will help us to conquer our enemies and to repair our losses. But it is not absolutely necessary that the cross should be worn; according to the rule, it may be replaced by a medal or a scapular of the Holy Face.

Aspirations Throughout the Day

May Thy Holy Name, O Lord, be known and blessed
in all times and places.

Blessed Virgin Mary, reign over us with thy Divine Son Jesus, Amen.

The Little Sachet
or the
Gospel
of the
Holy Name of Jesus

Given by our Lord, in detail to Sister Marie de Saint Pierre,
she composed the devotional object known as *"The Little Sachet"*.

It consists of a leaflet on which is printed the short Gospel of the
Circumcision which mentions the giving of the Name of "Jesus" to
our Savior; a picture of the Child Jesus; the initials of His Sacred
Name and some invocations intended to inspire confidence together
with the lines: **"When Jesus was named, Satan was disarmed."**

In honor of the five letters of the Sacred Name of "J E S U S" and
by virtue of His Five Precious Wounds, our Lord promised her to
all who wear this little Gospel:

1. Protection from lightning.
2. The grace to escape the snares of the devil.
3. Protection from a sudden and unprovided death.
4. The grace to lead a virtuous life.
5. The grace of final perseverance.

The Scapular of the Holy Face

The Scapular of the Holy Face is a small picture of the Adorable Face of Jesus, printed on linen, which the faithful wear with devotion, as a testimony of love towards our Lord and as a preservative against temptations and the dangers of the soul and body.

It may be fastened upon the scapular of Our Lady of Mount Carmel or upon any other that has already been received. It is not necessary to have recourse to a priest in order to receive it, and there is no liturgical form to be complied with. When taking it to wear, no other obligation is contracted than that of wearing it in a spirit of faith and of reparation. It consists of two pieces of white flannel connected by two cords of braid, etc.; upon one piece is attached a small copy of the Holy Face as on the Veil of St. Veronica, and upon the other the title which the Roman governor wrote over the Cross. Venerable Leo Dupont, in his zeal to multiply images of the Sorrowful Face of the Redeemer, revived this salutary devotion and distributed them all over France, particularly during the cholera visitations, and in return received innumerable letters from recipients, who considered it had been their preservation from the plague.

HOLY FACE CALENDAR
From the Archconfraternity Manual

The Feast of the Most Holy Trinity, first principle of the work, because of the sovereign homage rendered the Adorable Name of God three time holy.

Good Friday (Holy Hour 2p.m. – 3p.m.) the ever-memorable anniversary of the day when the Face of our Redeemer has suffered the most for love of us. The Holy Hour which recalls the time when the Suffering Face gave up the ghost upon the cross is the object of special devotion for the members of the Confraternity.

Easter Sunday, the Resurrection of Our Lord Jesus Christ, when it is customary at Rome for the Veil of St. Veronica to be publicly exposed in the presence of the Sovereign Pontiff.

The Holy Name of Jesus, on the Sunday between January 1st and the 6th, or if there is no Sunday, on January 2nd.

The Transfiguration of our Lord Jesus Christ, August 6th.

The Feasts of Our Lady of Dolors, the Friday in Passion Week and September 15th.

Our Lady of LaSalette, September 19th, (Her apparition in 1846; on her maternal bosom appeared the instruments of the Sacred Passion surrounding a Crucifix.)

St. Michael the Archangel, whose cry of love and faith, was a thunderbolt to Lucifer and the fallen angels, May 8th and September 29.

St. Veronica, whose heroic and tender example is given a place in the Sixth Station in the Way of the Cross, February 4th.

The principal feast of the Archconfraternity is that of St. Peter, Apostle, who was raised up after his fall by the compassionate look of the Holy Face, and who was the first to proclaim the glory and majesty of the Holy Name of Jesus. Also, it is in the Basilica of St. Peter in the Vatican that the Veil of St. Veronica is preserved and venerated.

St. Martin, Bishop of Tours, November 11th.

St. Louis, King of France, August 25th.

St. Teresa of Jesus, October 15th.

St. Therese of the Child Jesus and of the Holy Face, October 3rd.
   (New calendar October 1st)

St. Dismas, the Good Thief, April 24th.

The associates of the Archconfraternity are recommended to sanctify these feasts by special acts of reparation, Holy Communion, and by a visit to the Holy Face of our Divine Lord in a church or chapel where the Confraternity is canonically established.

FEAST OF THE HOLY FACE

On April 27th, 1910, Pope Saint Pius X approved the Feast of the Image of the Holy Face, with Rite of greater Double in the Third Feria, after the Sunday of Quinquaesima (Shrove Tuesday) for the diocese of Cambrai, France.

Holy Face Sources

Shrine of the Holy Face
Oratoire de La Sainte Face
8 Rue Bernard Palissy
37000 Tours, France

Send a letter to the above address to join the Archconfraternity of the Holy Face. Holy Face Medals, Pictures, Chaplets, Rosaries, etc., and Vials of Holy Face Oil are available.

Discalced Carmelite Monastery
of the Infant of Prague and St. Joseph
600 Flowers Ave.
Dallas, TX 75211
http://www.dallascarmelites.com/

Confraternity of the Holy Face meeting 3:30 p.m. every 1st Sunday. Confraternity meetings are open to the public.

For Presentations of the Holy Face Relic

Contact:

Joel and Donna Sue Berry
catholicpoet@att.net

P.O. Box 30661
Edmond, OK 73003

Bibliography

Veronica; or The Holy Face of Our Lord Jesus Christ, An Historical Notice of the Most Holy Relic of the Vatican Basilica of St. Peter. London: Thomas Richardson and Son, Dublin; and Derby. New York: Henry II. Richardson and Co. MDCCCLXX. http://www.holyfacedevotion.com/files/VeronicaOrTheHolyFaceOfJesusChrist-1872.pdf

The Devotion to the Holy Face at St. Peter's of the Vatican and in Other Celebrated Places. Re. Abbe Janvier. Tours Oratory of the Holy Face, Rue Bernard – Palissy, 8. 1888. http://www.holyfacedevotion.com/files/Devotion-to-the-Holy-Face-1888-Janvier.pdf

The Little Office of the Holy Face Manual. Sisters of the Divine Compassion. 1889. http://www.holyfacedevotion.com/files/LittleOfficeOfTheHolyFace-1889.pdf

The Holy Face in the Documents of the Church. Stefano Pedica, Marietti Editori Ltd. Italy 1960. http://www.holyfacedevotion.com/files/Holy-Face-in-Docs-of-the-Church-Pedica.pdf

The Message of Sister Mary of St. Peter. Louis Van Den Bossche. Carmel of Tours. Tours, France. 1953. http://www.holyfacedevotion.com/files/The-Message-of-Sr-Mary-of-St-Peter-Louis-Van-Den-Bossche.pdf

The Month of the Holy Face. Father Fourault, Priest of the Holy Face. Oration of the Holy Face, Tours, France. 1891. http://www.holyfacedevotion.com/files/Month%20Of%20The%20Holy%20Face%201891.pdf

Manual of the Archconfraternity of the Holy Face. Rev. Abbe Janvier, Dean of the Metropolitan Chapter of Tours, Priest of the Holy Face. Oratory of the Holy Face. 8 Rue Bernard – Palissy. 1887 http://www.holyfacedevotion.com/files/ManualoftheArchconfraternityoftheHolyFace.pdf

The Life of Leon Papin-Dupont, the Holy Man of Tours. Abbe' Janvier. London: Burns and Oates, Granville Mansions, Orchard Street. Dublin: M. H. Gill & Sons. 1882. http://www.holyfacedevotion.com/files/TheLifeofLeoDupont1882.pdf

Devotions to the Holy Face Booklet. 1890. Rev. Dean Kinane. Diocese of Cashel, Tipperary, Ireland. 1890. http://www.holyfacedevotion.com/files/Devotions%20to%20the%20Holy%20Face%201890.pdf

Janvier, M. L'Abbe, *Sister Mary St. Peter, Carmelite of Tours*. 1884.
http://www.holyfacedevotion.com/files/LifeofSisterMaryStPeter-1884.pdf

Rev. P. Janvier. *Sister Saint Pierre and the Work of Reparation*.
New York. Catholic Publication Society Co. 9 Barclay Street. London: Burns &
Oates, 28 Orchard St. 1885
http://www.holyfacedevotion.com/files/SrPierre-WorkofReparation-1885.pdf

Dublin Review. 1885. Vol. 97, PG. 78-102
http://www.holyfacedevotion.com/files/TheDublinReview-1885-TheHolyFace.pdf

Catholic Encyclopedia. St. Veronica.
http://www.newadvent.org/cathen/15362a.html

Jubilee Part II, St. Peter's.
http://www.adoremus.org/0500-St.Peter's.html

Veronica's Veil.
http://www.catholictradition.org/veronica.html

The Little Manual of the Confraternity of the Holy Face. 1936. 1973. Confraternity
of the Holy Face, Detroit, Michigan. (Out of print)

Scallan, Dorothy Scallan. *The Holy Man of Tours, The life of Leo Dupont.* Rockford,
Illinois. Tan Books and Publishers, Inc. 1990

Scallan, Rev. Emeric B. *Veronica's Veil.* New York. The William-Frederick Press.
1954.

Scallan, Rev. Emeric B. *The Golden Arrow (The Autobiography of Sister Mary of St. Peter.).*
New York. The William-Frederick Press. 1954.

Cruz, Joan Carroll. *Relics.* Huntington, Indiana. Our Sunday Visitor.

Devotion to the Holy Face of Jesus. Pamphlet.

Holy Face Devotion. This web site has a mountain of information on the Holy
Face Devotion. http://www.holyfacedevotion.com/index.htm

 *St. Veronica and the Holy Face.* Picture found among old family treasures.

 Veronica's Veil. True Image from an old prayer book.

 Sepia Veronica's Veil. True Image.

Tissot, James Jacques. *A Holy Woman Wipes the Face of Jesus.* 1836 - 1902. Brooklyn, New York.
https://commons.wikimedia.org/wiki/File:Brooklyn_Museum_-
_A_Holy_Woman_Wipes_the_Face_of_Jesus_(Une_sainte_femme_essuie_le_visage_
de_J%C3%A9sus)_-_James_Tissot.jpg

Preti, Mattia. Santa Veronica con il velo. 1613-1699. Rome, Taverna(Italia), Modena, Naples, Messina, La Valletta (Malta). Oil on canvas. https://en.wikipedia.org/wiki/Veil_of_Veronica#/media/File:Mattia_Preti_-_Santa_Veronica_con_il_velo.jpg

Mochi, Francesco. Statue of St. Veronica and the Veil. 1629. at St. Peter's Basilica. https://commons.wikimedia.org/wiki/File:Saint_veronica.jpg

Veronica's Veil Promises Pamphlet

American Colony (Jerusalem). *Interior of the house of St. Veronica.* 1900-1920. Dry plate negatives. Stereographs. G. Eric and Edith Matson Photograph Collection Repository. Library of Congress Prints and Photographs Division. Washington D. C.

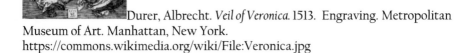Durer, Albrecht. *Veil of Veronica.* 1513. Engraving. Metropolitan Museum of Art. Manhattan, New York.
https://commons.wikimedia.org/wiki/File:Veronica.jpg

 St. Therese of the Child Jesus and of the Holy Face. Curtesy of Vickie Schreiner.

 Sr. Marie de St. Pierre. Old prayer book.

From friend Vicki Schreiner

The Veil of Veronica given to the author by the Carmelite Monastery in Dallas, Texas.

Privett, Jane Frances. *The Little Veronicas*. Sketch. 2018.

Privett, Jane Frances. *The Little Veronicas*. Sketch. 2018.

Privett, Jane Frances. *The Little Veronicas*. Sketch. 2018.

Venerable Leo Dupont.
https://fr.wikipedia.org/wiki/L%C3%A9on_Papin_Dupont#/media/File:L%C3%A9on_Papin_Dupont.jpg

Ven. Leo Dupont in death.

Ven. Leo Dupont

Holy Face according to St. Veronica's Veil. Author's picture.

 Veronica Coin. Photo owners - Jeremy and Monica Ingle. Editor/Owners Oremus Press. http://www.oremuspress.com/

 Vials of Blessed oil from the Shrine of the Holy Face in France.

Holy Face Devotion at St. Damien of Molokai Parish. Edmond, Oklahoma.

 Holy Face pamphlet.

Holy Face picture given to the author from the Dallas Carmelite Convent of the Infant of Prague and St. Joseph.

Chaplet of the Holy Face. Author's Chaplet. 2018.

  Holy Face Cross.

 The Little Sachet or the Gospel of the Holy Name of Jesus.

 The Holy Face Scapular.

About the Author

Born and raised in central Oklahoma in 1955, Donna Sue Berry is a wife, mother of two, and grandmother of twelve. She and retired rancher husband, Joel Doc, share their time between the wheat fields of Oklahoma and the mountains of Montana. Donna Sue began writing poetry and song lyrics soon after she first read Romeo and Juliet during junior high school. However, it wasn't until she enrolled in her freshman year at the University of Central Oklahoma (at age 47) that her poetry began to deepen and truly express her great love for Christ and her Catholic Faith. Her favorite poems are rhyming, story poems which weave around a person's thoughts and emotions. She says she writes with an Oklahoman's heart and accent.

She currently writes for Catholic newspaper, the OREMUS Press, on-line Regina Magazine, and her poetry has been published in Catholic Spiritual Direction. In fall 2017, she published two books, "The Seven Sorrows of the Blessed Virgin Mary" and "Our Souls, They Are Not Dead!" In 2018 "Veronica's Veil, Poems, Prayers, and Promises" was published a well as "Veronica's Veil, the Companion Prayer Book" and "Catholic Poems from the Heart of a Red Dirt Oklahoma Girl". Available at bookstores everywhere and Amazon or directly from: Berry Books Publishing, P.O. Box 30661, Edmond, OK. 73003

catholicpoet@att.net

https://catholicpoemsfromtheheartofareddirtoklahomagirl.com/

O God,
our Protector,
look on us, and look on the
Face of Thy Christ!

Made in the USA
Coppell, TX
07 June 2023

17809204R00079